HERBAL HOUSEPLANTS

HERBAL HOUSEPLANTS

Grow Beautiful Herbs—Indoors!

SUSAN BETZ

COOL
SPRINGS
PRESS

© 2021 Quarto Publishing Group USA Inc.

Text © 2021 Susan Betz

First Published in 2021 by Cool Springs Press, an imprint of The Quarto Group, 100 Cummings Center, Suite 265-D Beverly, MA 01915, USA. T (978) 282-9590 F (978) 283-2742 QuartoKnows.com

Cool Springs Press titles are also available at discount for retail, wholesale, promotional, and bulk purchase. For details, contact the Special Sales Manager by email at specialsales@quarto.com or by mail at The Quarto Group, Attn: Special Sales Manager, 100 Cummings Center, Suite 265-D, Beverly, MA 01915, USA.

ISBN: 978-0-7603-6955-5

Digital edition published in 2021 eISBN: 978-0-7603-6956-2

Library of Congress Control Number: 2020949466

Design: Debbie Berne Design Photography: Amy Kimball | amykimballphotography.com; except for pages 40, 41, 50, 52, 72, 74, 119, 124 (left), 126 (right), 131 (bottom) via Shutterstock Illustrations: Abby Diamond | @Finchfight

Printed in China

25 24 23 22 21   1 2 3 4 5

To my husband, David John Betz.

"Two are better than one because they have good return for their labor."
—Ecclesiastes 4:9

CONTENTS

INTRODUCTION

The herb becomes the teacher,
men stray after false goals,
when the herb he treads,
knows much, much more.
—Henry Vaughn, Seventeenth-Century Philosopher-Physician-Poet

What is an herb? Something for everyone!

There have been many definitions of the word "herb" offered by those interested in the subject; for some, the term brings to mind the plants, such as parsley, oregano, and chives, used in culinary dishes. Botanically speaking, it is a plant whose stem does not become "woody and persistent," an herbaceous plant that dies back to the ground in winter, but this obviously excludes some of the most common herbs—rosemary, thyme, and sage. Historically, it may be a plant valued for its medicinal purpose, flavor, or scent and now admired for its ornamental beauty in a flower border.

The Herb Society of America defines herbs as "plants, trees, shrubs, vines, perennials, biennials, or annuals valued historically, presently, or potentially for their flavor, fragrance, medicinal qualities, insecticidal qualities, economic or industrial use, or in the case of dyes, for the coloring material they provide." (Holly Shimizu, *Essential Guide to The Beginner's Herb Garden*) I define herbs as plants with possibilities.

The rising wellness trend these days isn't just about keeping the body healthy; it's also about nourishing the mind and spirit. Today, 50 percent of the world's population resides in an urban environment; consequently, younger generations find themselves with less personal space, time, and money, provoking a yearning for a deeper relationship with the natural world. Because of this, they are turning to indoor plants to provide some of those benefits.

More than purely decorative, herbs are patient, tolerant, companionable plants and have always been adept at multitasking in and out of a garden. Whether planted in a pot or a plot, herbs encourage a spirit of human creativity and offer a comforting connection to the natural world. They are not only useful plants, but they also personalize the people-plant connection. Good relationships are what give our lives meaning and herbs are great at making friends for themselves.

Herbs have influenced culture and tradition across generations for thousands of years, woven into the fabric of religion, mythology, and folklore in every land. Since the earliest recorded history, herbs have played a vital role in humankind's health and well-being. The captivating adventure of growing and using herbs is never-ending. Over time the various uses of plants change, as do our needs, and a list of useful plants will differ from culture to culture and vary from one generation to the next.

In 1969, Adelma Grenier Simmons, a leading twentieth-century authority on herbs, wrote *Herbs to Grow Indoors, for Flavor, for Fragrance, for Fun*, the first book of its kind on how to successfully grow herbs in the average home environment. Fifty years later, new techniques, efficient grow lights, and herb varieties specifically bred for compact spaces offer those in urban situations a better and easier way to grow these delightful plants indoors.

My purpose in writing about the herbs I love is to promote the peace and tranquility found in growing and loving them. I wish you the best as you explore the endless possibilities found in growing herbs indoors and the benefits for body and soul they provide.

1.
An Herbal Primer

PART 1

SUCCESS WITH HERBS INDOORS

There is no gardening without humility, an assiduous willingness to learn, and a cheerful readiness to confess you were mistaken. Nature is continually sending even its oldest scholars to the bottom of the class for some egregious blunder. But by the due exercise of patience and diligence they may work their way to the top again.
—**Alfred Austin,** *The Garden That I Love,* 1906

The evangelists of the plant kingdom, herbs give more for the time and space devoted to them than any other category of growing things. Everyone enjoys herbs in one form or another. They are among Mother Nature's oldest garden gifts. Herbs were the first plants welcomed indoors, not for aesthetic reasons, but out of necessity. History tells us that herbs were valued first for their medicinal qualities. Herbs also serve many useful functions in daily life, such as flavoring, fragrance, dyes, teas, insecticides, and other creative pursuits.

We often select plants based on their large or colorful flowers but the beauty of herbs is not subject solely to their flowers. Gardeners appreciate herbs for their attractive foliage colors, leaf textures, and fragrance. In a natural sense, there is no such thing as a "house plant," for no plant can claim a house as its natural habitat. A plant growing in a container depends on the gardener for its every need. To say growing herbs indoors is simple would be misleading. Not all herbs are suitable for indoor culture due to their size or unattractive growth habit.

Successful indoor herb gardening begins with choosing the right plants for the windows and other growing conditions in your home. Most herbs are sun lovers, so an unobstructed window facing south, west, or east is the best place to grow an indoor herb garden. A few plants will do well with good light and minimal sunlight, such as mint, myrtle, and lemon balm.

Given the variety and diversity of herbs available for cultivating indoors and outdoors, it is impossible to offer a standard set of cultural needs and care requirements that apply to all herbs. It is best to understand the individual needs of the particular plant you wish to grow and to meet those needs. In the plant profiles found in later chapters of this book, each plant species' specific needs are detailed to make the process easier.

An herb's native habitat offers valuable clues on how to grow it. Knowing the botanical classification or Latin name of a plant will help you correctly identify the plant and its origins. From that information, you can deduce some of its growth characteristics.

Herbs can be classified as *annual*, *biennial*, and *perennial*. Annuals have one season of growth, although some re-seed themselves. Cilantro is an excellent example of an annual herb. Biennials have two seasons of growth with flowers the second year. Parsley is a good example of a biennial herb. Perennials, some lasting years, have ongoing growth. Sage and thyme are perennial herbs.

Although there are many delightful myths and enchanting legends associated with growing herbs, the magical gift of a green thumb, unfortunately, is not one of them. Gardening is a skill developed through trial and error, and container gardening is an excellent way to begin cultivating your green thumb skills. All plants have four basic needs: sunlight, soil, water, and nutrients, each of which is discussed—as they pertain to herbal houseplants—in the next section. A green thumb is nothing more than a good understanding of plants and their requirements, plus the time, inclination, and determination to consistently meet those requirements.

PART 2
CARING FOR YOUR HERBS

Plants are nonjudgmental, nonthreatening, and nondiscriminating. They respond to care, not to the strengths or weaknesses of the person providing it. It does not matter if a person is black or white, has been to kindergarten or college, is poor or wealthy, healthy or ill. Plants will thrive when given careful attention.

—Charles L. Lewis, *Green Nature—Human Nature: The Meaning of Plants in Our Lives*

Light

Light is nourishment and energy to a plant. One of the most important aspects of growing herbs is making sure they get enough light. Herbs are sun lovers and need at least 5 to 6 hours of sunlight per day. If your plants are getting spindly and elongated, they are not receiving enough light and need a brighter window. Turn your plants regularly, so all sides get even exposure to light. Placing a plant just a few feet away from a window can reduce light intensity up to 50 percent.

Light conditions suitable for growing plants can be created virtually anywhere indoors using artificial illumination. A simple full spectrum grow light with a high level of light output will work for most herbs if window light isn't bright enough. Place the light 1 to 2 feet (30 to 60 cm) above the plant, depending on its size.

Plants need rest, too, so schedule your lights on an electric timer set for approximately 12 to 14 hours a day.

Temperature and Humidity

Herbs are happy in a typical home environment. Temperatures between 50°F and 70°F (10°C and 21°C) are ideal. Difficulties that arise with growing herbs indoors are often due to air that is too hot or dry, especially if the plants are sitting near hot air vents. One way to combat low humidity is to set your pots on top of a tray of gravel filled with water, making sure the bottoms of the containers are not sitting in water. Air-conditioning blowing directly onto plants will also rob moisture from the soil, so be mindful to locate your herbal houseplants away from air vents.

Misting your herbs once or twice a week with a plant sprayer will also help your herbs resist insect pests that thrive in dry, hot environments. Houseplants

like company, so grouping herbs about 5 inches (13 cm) apart from each another creates a beneficial microclimate that stimulates more fragrance and makes it easier to water. Just like people, herbs need fresh air. Open a window occasionally to give them some fresh air or use a fan to increase indoor air circulation.

Potting and Soil Mixtures

Many commercial potting soils are available for indoor gardening, including multipurpose peat-based mixes, soil-based blends, and others designed to suit specific plant needs, such as for cacti or orchids. Good drainage is essential for growing herbs and a soil pH that is neutral to slightly alkaline is best. The classic soil mixture for producing healthy, vigorous herbs contains these ingredients:

- 3 parts soil-based potting mix
- 1 part coarse sand
- 1 part compost
- 1 part perlite

Organic soil-based potting mixes hold more nutrients, especially trace elements, and retain their porous structure longer than peat-based blends. In general, these soil-based mixes are better for potted herbs.

With time, potting soil becomes depleted, breaks down, and plant roots become too crowded for the pot's size. Roots growing through the drainage holes and the need to water more frequently because the soil dries out quickly between waterings are hints that it's time to repot. To be sure repotting is necessary, turn a well-watered plant upside-down, tap the rim of the pot on a table, and remove the plant. If the plant is pot-bound, you will see a matted tangle of roots and not much soil. Repot the plant into a new pot that is 2 to 3 inches (5 to 7.5 cm) larger than its previous container. Lightly moisten the soil mixture a few hours before filling the pot. Center your plant and firm the soil around the stem or crown of the plant. Keep the soil level at least ½ inch (1 cm) below the rim of the pot. Always water plants thoroughly after transplanting.

There are two schools of thought regarding the repotting of houseplants. Some believe late winter or early spring, when new growth begins, is the proper time to repot herbal houseplants into fresh soil or a larger pot before they shift into active growth. In contrast, others insist it is better to repot in late summer before bringing the plants inside. Either way, most herbal houseplants should have fresh soil yearly, even if they are repotted in the same pots. Some experts recommend washing the old soil from the plant's roots before repotting it in fresh soil, but I find this isn't always necessary. I generally repot most of my potted herbs in spring and check them again in late summer. Occasionally there are a few that need to be repotted twice in the same year.

Choosing Containers

There is a fantastic variety of containers for cultivating indoor gardens, all with varying advantages or disadvantages. Whichever container you select for an herbal houseplant, it should suit the size and needs of the specific herb you plan to grow in it. The pot needs to be deep enough to accommodate the roots of the plant and wide enough to support the future growth of the plant. For example, parsley is a plant with a long taproot and requires a container that is deep enough to accommodate the length of its entire root structure.

Time and again, the merits of clay versus glazed or plastic pots are debated for growing plants indoors or outdoors. Aesthetics are important, but practicality is even more so. People like glazed or plastic pots for growing plants because the soil in them dries out less rapidly, but most herbs like "dry feet" and the soil in glazed or plastic pots is not as well-aerated as it is in porous containers like those made from clay (terra cotta).

Clay pots are preferable for growing herbs indoors because the growing conditions within the pot are easily adjusted by altering the type of soil used, the amount of drainage, or by adding or withholding water. They allow the potting soil in the pot to "breathe"

because the water slowly evaporates through the sides of the pot, increasing the air exchange between the soil and the roots. This means the plants are less apt to have wet feet, which can hinder (or worse!) their growth. What's more, the moisture evaporation through the porous sides of clay containers is a simple way to raise humidity and moisture in the air surrounding the plant.

Ornamental glazed pots do make beautiful temporary homes for seasonal displays or staging your herbs for special events or entertaining but herbs do not like wet feet. Placing a layer of pebbles in the bottom of a container with a waterproof base and no drainage holes will keep plant roots lifted out of any standing water in the bottom of the pot.

Saucers protect the surface under potted plants and prevent water stains on rugs and floors and damaged furniture. Use waterproof glazed rubber or glass pot saucers proportioned to the size of the pot. Because fertilizer salts leach from the potting soil with each watering, discard any water remaining in the saucer. Do not pour it back into the pot.

Watering

Learn to read the plant and it will tell you if it's thirsty. Proper watering and good drainage are essential for growing herbs. They are generally forgiving, but soggy soil is a sure prescription for root rot and fungal disease. How quickly a plant dries out indoors depends on the humidity level of the room it's in, the season, and the type of pot it's growing in. Plants that dry out quickly or have roots growing out through the drainage holes should be repotted. During winter, lower temperatures and shorter amounts of daylight decrease the need for water. Experience and observation will help determine when watering is necessary. Two easy ways to test the dryness level of the soil are to stick your finger into the soil to feel how dry it is and to lift the pot and test its weight. Wet soil weighs more than dry soil, so when the pot is very light, it's time to water.

Improper watering is the number-one killer when growing herbs indoors. To water the herbs, gently pour the water into the pot until it runs out of the drainage hole. After an hour or so, empty any standing water left in the pot saucer to avoid waterlogging the roots. Try to water your herbs early in the day, especially in winter, as watering indoor plants at night sometimes tends to encourage mold and fungus troubles.

Fertilizing

Use an organic half-strength solution of a 15-15-15 liquid fertilizer to feed your indoor herbs. Many indoor plant enthusiasts favor liquid fertilizers because watering and feeding are completed at the same time. All high-quality fertilizers have three numbers, which represent the three primary elements they contain that are essential for healthy plant growth—nitrogen, phosphorous, and potassium (NPK). Look at the fertilizer label to determine the percentage of each of these elements. I use a fish emulsion to fertilize my herbs every 2 or 3 weeks when they are actively growing. It fosters naturally occurring beneficial soil bacteria that are not of significant importance in many inorganic fertilizers. The lower temperatures and fewer daylight hours of late autumn and winter decrease the need for fertilizer, especially during periods of slow growth or dormancy. Gradually start fertilizing again when spring returns.

Herbs should be pruned regularly as they grow, pruning is key to the health and well-being of attractive, nicely shaped plants with lush foliage.

Pruning and Grooming Herbal Houseplants

Every herb species has its own growth habit and natural shape. Plants growing in containers require a little more grooming than those grown in the ground. Fast-growing plants, like herbs, need frequent pinching to promote maximum foliage production and deter straggly growth. Most herbs put on new growth at their branch tips, and this is where they should be snipped or pinched regularly to encourage a bushier form. Some herbs, such as chives, parsley, and sorrel, grow from the base of the plant; old growth should be removed from the sides of these plants rather than from the branch tips.

Plants grow from their leaves as well as the roots so be careful not to overprune your plants. In general, prune plants during periods of active growth, which means early spring through summer for most herbs, especially the woody varieties such as lavender, rosemary, sage, and thyme.

Propagating Herbs

In my garden there is a large place for senti-ment. My garden of flowers is also my garden of thoughts and dreams. The thoughts grow as freely as the flowers, and the dreams are as beautiful.

—**Abram L. Urban**, *The Voice of the Garden*

There are several ways to propagate herbs, whether they're grown as garden plants or as houseplants. Starting new plants from seed is one possible method but vegetative propagation techniques, such as taking stem cuttings or root divisions, are often faster. Let's discuss a few easy ways to make more herbs for your houseplant collection, or to share with friends and family.

SOWING SEEDS

Growing a plant from seed is an enjoy-ment shared by the novice and expert grower alike. Short-lived herbaceous herbs such as parsley, dill, basil, or sum-mer savory are easy to grow from seed. Seeds require a porous well-drained soil for best germination results, especially indoors. Small terra cotta pots filled with moist potting soil work well for sowing a few seeds at a time. Do not sow seeds too thickly or deeply. Check the seed packet for detailed directions. As a rule of thumb, plant a seed no deeper than three times the seed's diameter.

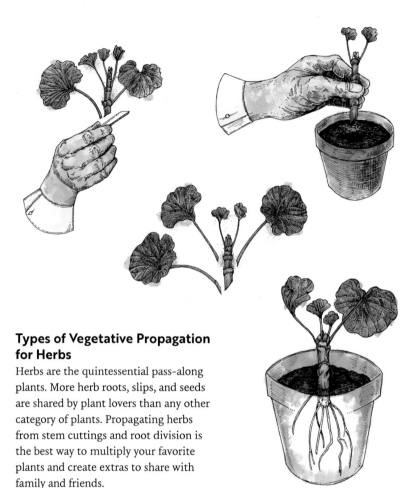

Types of Vegetative Propagation for Herbs

Herbs are the quintessential pass-along plants. More herb roots, slips, and seeds are shared by plant lovers than any other category of plants. Propagating herbs from stem cuttings and root division is the best way to multiply your favorite plants and create extras to share with family and friends.

CUTTINGS

One of the most effective ways to propagate plants is by taking cuttings. Cuttings can be taken from the leaves, shoots, or roots of a parent plant. These cuttings are then put into water or potting soil to form roots and become new plants. Plants reproduced this way are identical to the parent plant, which is why taking cuttings is a reliable way to propagate unusual varieties of herbs developed through hybridization or mutation. Late spring and summer, while plants are actively growing, are opportune times to take herb cuttings for houseplants because you can start them outdoors in their natural environment.

How to Take a Stem Cutting

To take cuttings of succulent-stemmed herbs such as scented geraniums, patchouli, and many others, make a clean diagonal cut with a sharp knife *just below* a node—the place where a leaf meets the stem—2 to 4 inches (5 to 10 cm) below the top of the stem. Cuttings from woody, shrubby herbs, such as lavender, rosemary, and thyme, should be taken from fresh new plant shoots and should measure about 4 inches (10 cm)

long. Use sturdy, nonflowering stems with lots of leaves.

Taking care not to tear the stem, remove all but the top two or three leaves, which will supply the plant with nutrients as the new root system develops.

Dip the bottom of the stem in rooting hormone, then gently insert the bottom end of the cutting into a container filled with moist potting soil. Keep the cutting watered well and do not move it from the container until the new roots measure ¼ to ½ inch (0.6 to 1 cm) long. When roots have formed, cuttings take on a fresh green appearance. The usual length of time required to root cuttings is 4 to 6 weeks. Cuttings from plants with woody stems tend to root more slowly.

ROOT DIVISION

Root division is a method of multiplying plants by splitting large mature plants into several smaller plants. Herbs that spread by broadening basal clumps, such as chives, mint, oregano, and thyme, or herbs that grow from underground rhizomes (fleshy horizontal stems), such as cardamom, are easily divided. In general, spring is the best time of year for root division of indoor plants. The newly divided plants will have ample time to establish a solid root system and healthy foliage over summer before moving back inside for winter.

How to Make a Root Division

Remove the plant from its pot, shake the soil from the roots, and carefully pull apart or separate sections from the clump of roots. Repot each root section in a new container. Water each new plant well and keep them in moderate light for 2 to 4 weeks. Herbs such as mint, catnip, chives, lemon balm, and most oreganos can be divided like this to create new plants.

HELPFUL TOOLS AND SUPPLIES FOR INDOOR GARDENERS

Good gardening is doing what should be done when it should be done, whether you feel like doing it or not. Having the proper tools for cultivating your indoor plants will increase the enjoyment and ease of growing and tending your herbs.

· Environmentally friendly insecticide and disease-control products

· Liquid fertilizer: fish emulsion, kelp, or seaweed

· Plant mister

· Plant trays and pebbles

· Pocket snips

· Potting soil

· Pots of various sizes

· Rooting hormone

· Small fan for circulating air

· Small trowel or old kitchen fork and spoon

· Watering can with a long spout for reaching among plants and water control

PART 3
KEEPING YOUR HERBAL HOUSEPLANTS HEALTHY

Take care of your herbs and your herbs will take care of you.

Pests and Cultural Problems

When it comes to pest and disease control, the best defense is a good offense. To keep your plants happy and stress-free, examine them frequently. Stay ahead of insects and disease by recognizing early symptoms of trouble. By improving the plant's way of life, you can usually restore it to robust health.

COMMON HERBAL HOUSEPLANT PESTS

Aphids
Aphids—small, oval-shaped, leaf-sucking insects—vary in color from green, pink, and black to dusty gray, or even with a fluffy white coating. Aphid colonies reproduce and multiply quickly. Nymphs look like adults but lack wings. Aphids suck water and nutrients from the leaves and stems of a plant and carry viruses they pass from plant to plant as they feed.

Signs/Symptoms: Curled or wilted foliage and stunted growth are good indicators of aphids. Aphids are especially fond of tender, young leaf tips and flower buds. The plant may look frail and wasted and a sticky honeydewlike substance accumulates on leaves.

ORGANIC PESTICIDE AND FUNGICIDE CONTROL

This hydrogen peroxide solution, in addition to controlling aphids, is also useful as a foliage spray to control fungus gnats and spider mites. Occasionally watering your plants with a diluted solution of hydrogen peroxide will boost oxygen levels and soil aeration. Let the soil dry briefly before resuming your regular watering regimen.

In a 24-ounce (720 ml) plastic or glass spray bottle, combine 2 cups (480 ml) water and 2 tablespoons (30 ml) 3 percent hydrogen peroxide. Cap the bottle and store at room temperature.

Treatment: Wash off aphids with water, or spray with a hydrogen peroxide solution, insecticidal soap, or horticultural oil. Repeat as necessary.

- For best growth in winter, do not allow herbs to produce flowers, except for scented geraniums and rosemary. Snip out the flower buds and the plant will devote its energy to creating more and better leaves.

- Plants, like people, take exception to chemically treated water. Use rainwater or filtered water for watering your herbs. If you live in an urban area with chlorinated tap water, fill a gallon glass container with water and let it sit for a few hours before watering the herbs. The chlorine will dissipate into the air and bring the water to room temperature. Your plants will thank you.

- A time-honored gardening tradition says the roots of newly potted plants will stick to the sides of wet or dirty clay pots, causing trouble when it's time to repot the plant. Therefore, clean, dry containers are always best. Before planting in a new clay pot, soak it in water for several hours to saturate the clay so it will not leach moisture from the planting medium.

- If growing several herbs together, choose plants with contrasting heights, leaf colors, shapes, and textures. Be sure to select herb varieties that have the same sun, soil, and water requirements.

- From time to time, it is helpful to cultivate a potted plant. Gently stir the soil surface in the pot with an old kitchen fork to introduce oxygen and break up crusty soil surfaces so water can penetrate more evenly.

- Keep a plant mister handy and frequently spray your plants to encourage growth and keep their leaves dust-free. To really stimulate plant growth and deep green foliage, occasionally mist them with sparkling water.

- Fresh air is essential for all living things, especially plants. On warm sunny days, open a window for a few minutes and let some fresh air into the house.

- Herbs offer people a fascinating, friendly, tasty, and safe way to explore cultural, geographic, and economic diversity. They kindly nurture and teach us that there are countless approaches of relating, knowing, and understanding the people-plant connection.

- Plants that only receive light from a window must be turned regularly to encourage healthy, evenly balanced growth of stems and leaves. This keeps the plant from growing leggy on one side.

- Understanding the lifecycle of a plant will help you plan for its future, accept when it's kaput, and let it depart in peace. It is also wise to learn to recognize when it's time to trash a pest-ridden or sick plant to stop further spread.

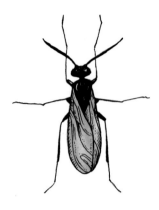

Fungus Gnats

More bothersome than harmful, fungus gnats resemble tiny blackish-brown fruit flies. The white larvae they produce inhabit the soil surface.

Signs/Symptoms: Gnats found flying about the plant and room, especially after the plant is disturbed, are your first clue there is a problem. The larvae feed on the organic matter in the soil but they also occasionally eat new roots, causing overall plant decline and fatigue. The adults do not feed on plants.

Treatment: Fungus gnats thrive in overly damp soil conditions. Increase air circulation around the plant with a fan and water the plant from the bottom. Let the soil dry out completely between waterings.

Mealy Bugs

Clusters of soft-bodied, wingless pests masked in white cottony fluff attached to the underside of plant leaves and stuck in stem crevices.

Signs/Symptoms: At first glance, mealy bugs are often mistaken for fungus or plant mold. Check plant for yellowing and wilting, curling leaves, and sticky honeydew-like secretions to confirm a mealy bug infestation.

Treatment: Wipe off leaves manually with a wet cotton ball and spray the herb with insecticidal soap or horticultural oil. Repeat as needed.

Spider Mites

Spider mites resemble tiny, fast-moving reddish-brown spiders and are barely visible to the naked eye. They crawl around the undersides of leaves.

Signs/Symptoms: Spider mites are indicated if you see a pale or yellow mottled cast to the plant's leaves, or notice leaf curling and dropping. Mites accumulate on the undersides of leaves, and in heavy infestations you can see faint tiny red pinpricks on the leaves. Delicate webs may cover the undersides of leaves and growing leaf tips.

Treatment: Spider mites especially dislike humidity and low room temperature. Spray with insecticidal soap or horticultural oil. Repeat as needed.

Whitefly

Whiteflies are present if you see tiny white insects on leaves and stems and shake the plant and clouds of insects rise and flutter around the foliage. Larvae and nymphs suck plant sap.

Signs/Symptoms: If your plant is dropping yellow leaves with sticky honeydewlike secretions on them, followed by black sooty mold, it's time for treatment.

Treatment: Spray the herb with insecticidal soap or horticultural oil. Repeat in 3-day intervals.

Plant Culture Problems

Sometimes a plant's health is negatively affected by the way it's cared for. Here are some cultural problems that might crop up when tending an herbal houseplant.

Problem	Symptoms	Solution
Bacterial or fungal disease	Brown, yellow, or black spots, spread by moisture and poor air circulation	Reduce watering, keep foliage dry, and improve air circulation. Clean away dead and dying parts of plants as soon as possible.
Brown leaf tips, drooping leaves, curled leaf tips	Temperature fluctuations, or watering a plant with cold water can cause trouble.	If plants are in a window during a sudden cold spell, draw the curtains or place a thick piece of cardboard against the window to keep the cold air from injuring tender foliage. Water with room-temperature water.
Lack of sunlight	Undersized new leaves and stems bending and leaning toward the light	Move the plant to a sunnier window or provide artificial light.
Low humidity	Shriveled leaves, curled, browned, or brittle leaves	Raise the humidity level around the plant.
Nutrient deficiency	Leaves that look pale and yellow can be a sign of nitrogen or iron deficiency.	Fertilize plants during the growing season, which for most herbs, begins in early spring and ends in fall.
Overwatering	Yellowing and dropping leaves, pale foliage, or tan blotches on foliage; fungus gnats on soil surface	Let plants dry out between waterings.
Wilting leaves	Overwatering or underwatering—in either case, the plant is not absorbing water. Dry soil caused by lack of water or waterlogged soil leads to wet, oxygen-deprived soil conditions and root rot.	Check drainage and adjust watering.

Helping Herbal House Plants Adapt to Seasonal Transition

There is a tender balance between knowledge and observation that is necessary to achieve a healthy garden. There is a rhythm to the seasons, but never a sameness.

—Thomas DeBaggio, *The Herb Companion*, 1989

Encourage your indoor herb plants to follow the natural rhythm of the seasons. Plants naturally thrive and grow in spring and summer, then slow their growth in fall and winter. Strive to make their seasonal environmental transition as gentle as possible.

SUMMERING HERBAL HOUSEPLANTS OUTDOORS

Watch for signs of new growth in early spring. When daylight hours begin to increase, make a light application of fertilizer and begin to increase the amount and frequency of waterings. Once the danger of frost has passed in your region, move potted herbs outdoors for summer.

Herbs that live indoors are incredibly tender compared to outdoor plants. Their leaves are fragile and they are easily damaged by sun or wind. When it's time to move your plants outside, help them acclimate by hardening them off the same way you would do with a seedling you have grown. Slowly acclimate your herbal houseplants to the outdoors by increasing the amount of time they spend outside by a few hours every day until they're outdoors full time. Start with just 1 to 2 hours a day and increase the time from there.

Remember the herbs' light requirements. Choose an appropriate site for each type of plant according to its demand for light. One benefit of growing your favorite herbs in containers is the ease with which they can be moved about outdoors to a location they will be happiest whether in sunlight or light shade.

Spring is also a good time to repot plants you want to grow larger or move into bigger pots as needed. They will have all summer to put on new growth. Keep your herbs fertilized and turn the pots occasionally to discourage uneven growth.

A collection of potted herbs moved outdoors in spring will give your porch or patio a decorative green touch and keep them close at hand for snipping or fragrance.

BRINGING PLANTS INDOORS FOR WINTER

Late summer is an excellent time to begin preparing your outdoor herbs for their move indoors. Debugging is an essential task to perform before bringing plants inside for winter. Check the leaves, stems, and soil for insects or disease. Wash and scrub the outsides of pots. Pay attention to the pot rims where insects can hide. Several weeks before transferring plants from the garden or patio to the house, spray plants for possible aphid, whitefly, or spider mite infestation with an insecticidal soap, making sure to cover all sides of the leaves. Repeat as needed to avoid bringing pests or their eggs inside.

You can travel the world in a windowsill garden of herbs. Keep in mind these plants are not only ornamental houseplants but are also helpful plants. Now that you are more familiar with the necessary cultural information on growing herbs indoors, it's time to look at some of the best herbs for indoor growing. I begin with culinary herbs, explore herbs for fun and fragrance, talk about the beautiful world of old-fashioned scented geraniums, and finish with temporary houseplants. The rest is up to you!

SPECIAL CONSIDERATIONS

· Divide and repot chives and mints and let them freeze before bringing them inside. Freezing provides a rest period and new growth produced afterward is firm and fresh.

· Annual herb plants, such as cilantro and basil, that have been growing all summer long, are reaching the end of their natural life cycle. Start new seedlings outdoors in late summer for a fresh vigorous supply of plants to bring indoors to grow and use throughout winter.

· Take root cuttings of tender perennial herbs and scented geraniums that have grown too large over the summer to bring back inside and start new plants from these cuttings.

· Lightly prune marjoram, rosemary, sage, and thyme, leaving just enough foliage so the plant does not go dormant. It takes time for these plants to recover from the move and you want your plants to flourish as they transition to spending winter indoors.

2.
Herbs for the Kitchen and Beyond

Though your garden for flowers doth in a sort peculiarly challenge itself a perfect and exquisite form to the eyes, yet you may not altogether neglect this, where your herbs for the pot do grow.
—William Lawson, *The Country Housewife's Garden,* 1617

Growing an indoor kitchen garden lets you enjoy the fragrance and flavor of fresh herbs year-round. There is something for everyone; the novice and gourmet chef alike appreciate how natural and delicious herbs enhance even the simplest meals, pleasing the eye as well as the palate. With today's emphasis on health and wellness, fresh herbs make great substitutes for processed seasonings and salt. They add zest to drinks, salads, main dishes, sweets, and soups.

Many common kitchen herbs are also valued and used for their health benefits: to calm stress, ease digestion, and build immunity by promoting overall wellness. Within the broad concept of what, precisely, an herb is, it's challenging to place them into distinct categories. The herbs have a multiplicity of uses—culinary, medicinal, fragrance, decorative, and more. From this point, individual tastes and interests will guide you in deciding which herbs to grow.

Chives

Allium spp.

Common chives

It's time the lilies of the kitchen received starring roles and the applause they so richly and deliciously deserve.
—**Barbara Batcheller, *Lilies of the Kitchen: Recipes Celebrating Garlic, Onion Leeks, Shallots, Scallions, and Chives***

Chives are members of the onion family—one of the most popular and widespread culinary flavorings in the world. Native to Asia, chives have been used as a culinary seasoning for almost 5,000 years. Explorer Marco Polo brought chives to Europe in the late thirteenth century where they rapidly became indispensable. Romanian gypsies used chives in their fortune-telling rites and an old British tradition suggests hanging clumps of chives over your doorway to drive away diseases and evil influences. There are no extensive medical uses recorded using chives, although they are said to aid the digestion of fatty foods. Chives are an essential ingredient in *fines herbes*, a finely chopped blend of herbs used for seasoning.

Chives are a great herb for a beginning herb enthusiast and an ideal candidate for indoor kitchen gardens. They develop quickly and produce in profusion, so you always have a few extra plants to share or set in your flower or vegetable garden. Chives seldom flower indoors, but a fringe benefit of growing them outdoors is their beautiful cluster of star-like edible flowers that bloom in shades of pink and white.

■ HERBAL LIFE

Common chives (*Allium schoenoprasum*) and garlic chives (*A. tuberosum*) are two of the best varieties for an indoor herb garden.

■ LIVING WITH CHIVES

Common names: allium, chives, rushleeks

Floral language: usefulness; "Why do you weep?"

Description: Hardy perennials, chives grow in clumps with small bulbs, or roots, that produce hollow, green onion-flavored spears and sweet round lilac flowers. Their Asian cousins, garlic chives, have flat, garlic-scented leaves and fragrant starlike white flowers. Indoors chives seldom bloom and reach 8 to 12 inches (20 to 30 cm) in height.

Growing conditions: Chives need strong sunlight, so place your plant in a south or bright west window. Plants like moist, well-drained soil. Prune yellowing leaves from the sides of plant. Chives should be repotted each summer and left outside to freeze before you bring them indoors.

Propagation: Chives are best propagated by seeds or root division.

Plant parts used: leaves; flowers are also edible

Garlic chives

Harvesting & preserving: Chives have a mild oniony flavor. Cut and use chives frequently, harvesting the base of outside leaves. Fresh chopped chives are supreme when added to soups, salads, cream cheese, butter, eggs, and mashed potatoes. Leaves can be refrigerated in a sealed bag for up to 5 days, or frozen in airtight containers for 2 to 3 months.

Pests: Chives are not often bothered by pests.

Aloe vera
Aloe barbadensis

If any one plant can be called America's folk remedy, it is aloe vera; every windowsill deserves one.
—**Steven Foster, *The Herb Companion*, February/March 1995**

Aloe vera is a tender, succulent perennial herb native to Africa. The earliest known reference to aloe is a depiction in a cave painting in South Africa. The word *aloe* is the Greek name for "plant," adapted from one of its ancient Arabic names, *alloeh*. *Vera* is Latin for "true." The plant's long documented history of use treating burns and internal inflammation dates back some 4,000 years. Reputed to be one of Cleopatra's beauty secrets, aloe vera is still used extensively in commercial cosmetics, hand creams, suntan lotions, and shampoos. Aloe is often described as "a drug store in a flowerpot" because of its healing virtues. The gel in the plant's long, tapering green leaves is a balm for healing cuts, burns, and other skin blemishes.

The dried leaf of aloe vera has a history of use as a bitter medicine for cathartic purposes and preventing hair loss. As a rub, the juice is used in Mexico to protect children from insect bites. French herbalists thought it was unlucky to see aloe blooming during the day, but in the evening, it was considered lucky. There are few plants as easy and decorative to grow as aloe; it practically thrives on neglect. Overwatering and poor drainage are the greatest threats to this plant.

■ **HERBAL LIFE**

According to folklore, growing aloe on your windowsill is believed to guard against evil and prevent household accidents.

■ **LIVING WITH ALOE**

Common names: burn plant, first-aid plant, medicine plant

Floral language: grief; religious superstition

Description: Aloe is an excellent indoor plant. On average the plant grows 2 feet (60 cm) tall and 1 foot (30 cm) wide. Its thick translucent succulent leaves with soft marginal spines grow in a fan-shaped clump. It can take several years for aloe to bloom. When it does, a leafless blossom stalk rises above the leaves to bear yellow or reddish racemes of bell-like flowers.

Growing conditions: Aloe grows best in a bright window, out of direct sunlight, in a well-drained sandy potting soil. Though its juice will soothe sunburn, the plant does not do well in direct sunlight. The leaves will turn reddish and burn if overexposed to the sun.

Propagation: Aloe vera plants are easily propagated. Remove the small suckers growing at the base of the mother plant, place them in potting soil in pots, and they will take root.

Plant parts used: Fresh leaves. Split open an aloe leaf and use the fresh gel to soothe chapped hands, dermatitis, insect bites, and burns.

Harvesting & preserving: Cut and harvest the lower outside leaves of the plant, not the young foliage from the center of the plant.

Pests: aphids, spider mites

Cilantro

Coriandrum sativum

Cilantro belongs to the *Apiaceae*, or parsley, family. Anise, caraway, chervil, cumin, dill, and fennel are a few other well-known family members. Cilantro is both an herb and a spice and its varied uses are based on different parts of the plant. Cilantro is the Spanish word used for the plant's strongly scented bright-green foliage. It is also called Chinese parsley due to its long history of use in Thai and Chinese cuisines. *Coriander* refers to the dried seed, or fruit, of the plant, rather than the fresh leaves, and is considered a spice.

The Chinese used the herb as far back as the Han dynasty in 206 BC and believed that the seeds bestowed eternal life upon those who consumed them. Greek and Roman physicians, including Hippocrates, made medicines from cilantro. The plant traveled to Britain with the Romans where it was cultivated in monastery gardens during the Middle Ages. Today it is a popular ingredient in salsa.

And the manna looked like small coriander seed, and it was pale yellow like gum resin. —**Numbers 11:7, NLT Bible**

Cilantro is native to southern Europe and the Mediterranean. The botanical name *Coriandrum* is derived from the Greek *koris*, meaning a bug, referring to what some consider a rank bedbug-like smell of the plant's leaves and unripe seeds. Cilantro is known by similarly odious words the world over, testifying to the plant's long association with humankind and extensive growing range—from central and southern Europe, Asia, and India to parts of North and South America.

■ HERBAL LIFE

Best indoor varieties and cultivars are 'Slow-Bolt' and 'Long Standing'.

■ LIVING WITH CILANTRO

Common names: Chinese parsley, cilantro, coriander

Floral language: hidden merit; "Your closeness is welcome."

Description: Cilantro is a short-lived annual and typically lasts from 8 to 10 weeks indoors. Strongly scented bright-green leaves resemble Italian parsley, then grow fernlike and jaggedly cut before developing clusters of small white flowers. Cilantro grows from a slender taproot and resents being transplanted.

Growing conditions: Place in direct bright sunlight for 5 to 8 hours a day, or use artificial lights. Cilantro grows best in loose, well-draining soil. Keep the soil moist but not consistently wet and provide good ventilation. Keep the pot on the cooler side to encourage lush foliage.

Propagation: Cilantro does best indoors if grown from seed planted in a deep pot to accommodate the plant's long taproot.

Plant parts used: leaf blades; seeds (known as coriander)

Harvesting & preserving: Harvest fresh leaves before the leaves turn feathery and the plant begins to flower. Cilantro leaves are best fresh; this herb does not keep its flavor when dried. Use the fresh leaves for seasoning salsas, salads, dips, and stir-fries.

Pests: aphids, fungus gnats, whiteflies

Lemongrass

Cymbopogon citratus

The lemon herbs are a large and highly varied group of plants that are members of many different plant families. They come from all corners of the globe, yet they so wonderfully mimic, in a variety of ways, the aroma and taste of lemon citrus.
—Henry Flowers, 2006

A semi-hardy perennial grass native to tropical Asia, lemongrass is a lovely lemon-scented herb closely resembling its cousin pampas grass in growth habit. It easily adapts to indoor conditions and makes a stunning useful fragrant accent plant when provided proper light and nutrients. Lemongrass has a long history of use as a food ingredient, in cosmetics, and as folk medicine, dating back some 2,000 years.

Lemongrass's aromatic oil contains large amounts of citral and geranium, a beautiful blend of lemon and rose scents highly prized commercially for use in soaps, perfumes, candles, and mosquito and insect repellents. Planted in hedge rows in India, it is reputed to repel tigers. When crushed, the smooth thin leaf stalks produce a rich lemon flavor traditionally used to season a variety of South Asian–inspired dishes, such as curries, soups, and poultry. Lemongrass is called *takrai* in the Thai language. A lemongrass plant makes a great focal point in a container garden with other lemon-scented herbs.

■ HERBAL LIFE

To make lemon-herb water: In a large glass container or carafe, combine 5 or 6 lemon slices, 5 or 6 fresh crushed lemongrass stalks, ½ cup (18 g) fresh lemon basil leaves, and ½ cup (18 g) fresh orange mint leaves. Cover everything with water and refrigerate for 12 to 24 hours. Strain and serve the flavored water in a glass pitcher with a few sprigs of fresh herbs.

■ LIVING WITH LEMON GRASS

Common names: fever grass, serai makan, West Indian lemongrass

Floral language: submission, utility, zest

Description: Lemongrass is a dense, clump-forming, lemon-scented plant with an erect growth habit and long, narrow grasslike leaves with prominent midveins and insignificant flowers. It can reach 2 to 3 feet (60 to 90 cm) tall.

Growing conditions: Direct sunlight is best. A south-facing window is an excellent location for this plant. Always provide good drainage and never allow the soil to dry out completely. Reduce watering in the winter. Lemongrass will soon outgrow its pot and need to be repotted. Heavily prune the plant in late winter to encourage fresh growth.

Propagation: Lemongrass is easily propagated by division or stem cuttings. It's a great pass-along plant for fellow indoor gardening enthusiasts.

Plant parts used: Use leaves, fresh or dried, in cold drinks, salads, and as a hot tea to ease stress.

Harvesting & preserving: The swollen base of the leaf stalk is used fresh. The leaves have sharp edges so be careful when harvesting.

Pests: spider mites; occasionally plant diseases such as rust and root rot

Bay
Laurus nobilis

A crown of bay good fortune brings to poets, cooks, scholars, and kings.
—**Carolyn Dille and Susan Belsinger,** *Herbs in the Kitchen*

Bay laurel is an ancient, aromatic evergreen shrub or tree native to the Mediterranean region. Dense and rather bushy in its growth habit, bay produces dark, glossy, green lance-shaped leaves that are both beautiful and useful. Yellow flowers emerge in the axils of stems, but bay seldom blooms indoors. Bay is valued for both culinary and ornamental purposes. If you like to cook, and considering the price of bay leaves,

having your own bay tree is an excellent investment. Adaptable and easygoing, bay tolerates indoor conditions better than most herbs and is a very striking summer patio plant.

Sweet bay is sometimes confused with the California bay (*Umbellularia californica*) native to the United States. Although it has similar characteristics, it is not a true laurel. When you crush a bay laurel leaf, you get a mild sweet nutmeg scent with hints of camphor. In contrast, a crushed California bay leaf has a strong menthol fragrance.

Bay laurel is the herb of classical literature. In Greek mythology, the beautiful nymph Daphne was transformed into a bay tree while being pursued by Apollo, the Greek god of prophecy, poetry, and healing. In honor of the tree, he decreed that poets, victors, and all who create beauty should be given a laurel wreath as their reward. Bay leaves are used to repel fleas, roaches, lice, and will prevent moths and bugs when placed in canisters of flour or grains.

■ HERBAL LIFE

Bouquet garni: An herb bouquet of fresh or dried herbs tied together and added to a dish while cooking then removed and discarded before the dish is served. Bay leaf, parsley, and thyme make a good bouquet garni combination.

■ LIVING WITH BAY

Common names: Grecian bay, sweet bay, true bay

Floral language: glory; "my feelings will change only with death"

Description: Bay is a tender perennial evergreen shrub or tree with elegant, smooth bark and evergreen leaves. The plant reaches 3 to 6 feet (90 to 180 cm) in height when cultivated in a pot indoors.

Growing conditions: Choose a bright sunny window and plant bay in a well-drained potting soil. Bay prefers to be watered regularly. Repot your bay plants every 2 to 3 years because they frequently become pot bound.

Propagation: Growing bay from seeds or stem cuttings is best, but it does require patience.

Plant parts used: Use the leaves fresh or dried. Use bay leaf in custards, fish

dishes, with meat, in soups and stews, and other foods. It's also decorative and fragrant in wreaths and potpourri.

Harvesting & preserving: When harvesting fresh bay leaves, do not pick single leaves. Instead, cut stem pieces several inches long and remove all the leaves for harvest. The plant will then send out two new branches. Fresh bay leaves refrigerated in an unsealed zipper-top bag will keep for several months.

Pests: Scale is a common pest problem on bay.

Horehound

Marrubium vulgare

Native to Asia and Europe, horehound has been valued for thousands of years as an herbal cough remedy. The botanical name of white horehound, *Marrubium* is a Hebrew derivation of the word *marrob*, meaning "bitter juice." On the other hand, the Romans esteemed horehound's medicinal properties and some authors say its Latin name is said to be derived from *Maria Urbs*, an ancient town of Italy.

White horehound is distinguished from other horehound species by its downy stem and densely felted hairs covering the leaves and calyx shape. The Greek physician Hippocrates, and many other herbalists, have held this plant in great regard down through the ages. It was also brewed and made into horehound ale, a tasty healthful alcohol-free beverage drunk in the United States, Australia, and England.

Syrup made of the greene fresh leaves and sugar is a most singular remedie against the cough and wheezing of the lungs . . . and doth wonderfully and above credit ease such as have been long sicke of any consumption of the lungs, as hath beene often proved by the learned physitions of our London College. **—John Gerard, English Herbalist**

Horehound is one of the five plants stated by the Mishna to be the "bitter herbs," which the Jews were ordered to take for the Feast of the Passover. **—Richard Folkard**

▣ LIVING WITH HOREHOUND

Common names: white horehound

Floral language: frozen kindness, health

Description: Horehound is a tender herbaceous perennial herb with a spreading habit and soft crinkled heart-shaped gray-green leaves borne on fuzzy square stems. Nondescript white flower clusters, growing in whorls at intervals along the stems, appear in summer. The plant reaches 12 to 18 inches (30 to 45 cm) in height indoors.

Growing conditions: When growing horehound indoors, provide bright light, including direct sunlight, and alkaline soil. Horehound is moderately tolerant of dry soil conditions, so you can let the soil dry out between waterings. Prune the plant regularly. Horehound is short lived; replace the plants annually, or as needed.

Propagation: easily raised from seed, division, or stem cuttings

Plant parts used: leaves, fresh and dried

Harvesting & preserving: Hang leaf bunches to dry. Once dry, horehound leaves can be stored in a glass jar away from light until needed. The flowers also dry well for flower arrangements.

Pests: none

HOREHOUND COUGH DROPS

3 cups (192 g) fresh horehound leaves

3½ cups (840 ml) water

2 tablespoons (28 g) butter, plus more for the baking sheet

3 cups (600 g) sugar

1. In a medium pot over low heat, simmer the horehound leaves in the water for 10 to 15 minutes.

2. While the horehound simmers, coat a baking sheet with butter and set aside.

3. Using a fine-mesh strainer set over a heatproof bowl, strain the leaves from the liquid and return the liquid to the pot. Discard the leaves.

4. Add the sugar and butter to the liquid infusion and simmer over medium heat until the liquid reaches a hard ball stage (300°F, or 150°C) on a candy thermometer. Immediately pour the hot mixture onto the prepared sheet. This candy only takes a minute or so to set, so quickly and deeply score the candy sheet with a knife into bite-size squares. After about 5 minutes, the candy will be completely hardened. Break it into small pieces along the score lines and store in an airtight container at room temperature for up to 6 months.

Lemon Balm
Melissa officinalis

Balm makes the heart merry and joyful.
—Arabian proverb

Native to the Mediterranean, lemon balm has been cultivated for more than 2,000 years and is found growing over much of the world today. A cousin of the kitchen garden mints, lemon balm has a rich history of cultural, medicinal, and culinary use. The genus name, *Melissa*, is derived from the Greek word for "honeybee." It was a favored plant of ancient beekeepers, who rubbed fresh lemon balm leaves inside their beehives to encourage bees to return to the hive and bring their friends.

One of the most sweetly scented of all herbs, lemon balm's crinkly heart-shaped leaves release a pleasing lemony-mint fragrance when gently brushed. In Elizabethan England, lemon balm was a favorite herb in nosegays and many gardeners and flower arrangers still enjoy the sweet perfume it adds to a fresh flower bouquet. Fresh lemon balm leaves lend a citrus tang to iced tea, green and fruit salads, wine, and fruit drinks. Add lemon balm sprigs to tarragon vinegar for an extra-special twist.

It is the herb's medicinal qualities that have earned it the most respect through the ages. "Heart's delight" and "elixir of life" are two descriptive names attributed to the herb's calming and restorative effects on the mind, body, and spirit. Lemon balm makes a delightfully soothing warm tea and aromatherapists recommend lemon balm to counter depression, anxiety, and insomnia. Growing in a sunny window or under a light in the bathroom, it will freshen the room. Toss some of the leafy tips into your bath water for a relaxing sensory experience. Once you have tasted and used this refreshing herb, you will not want to be without it.

■ **HERBAL LIFE**

For a joyful tea blend, combine lemon balm, sweet marjoram, apple mint, and peppermint.

■ **LIVING WITH LEMON BALM**

Common names: balm, bee balm, Melissa

Floral language: sharpens wit and understanding, healing, love, fun, rejuvenation

Description: Lemon balm is a bushy herbaceous perennial with upright branching stems that can reach 3 feet (90 cm) in height. Attractive, slightly heart-shaped, crinkly bright-green, mintlike leaves with serrated edges. Lemon balm has lovely lemon-scented leaves and insignificant white flowers that grow on one side of the square stem. Indoors, keep lemon balm pruned to 1 foot (30 cm) tall and 1 foot (30 cm) wide to discourage flowering.

Growing conditions: The best exposure is in a south or bright west window. Lemon balm requires 4 to 6 hours of direct sun each day. Cut the plant back when it gets leggy or too tall. Turn the pot regularly so all sides get even exposure to light. Use good potting soil

with a little horticultural sand mixed in to increase drainage. Water when the top of the soil begins to feel dry.

Propagation: Lemon balm is easily propagated by taking leaf cuttings, dividing the plant, or from seed.

Plant parts used: leaves, fresh or dried

Harvesting & preserving: Harvest the leaves for use in cold drinks, salads, and as a hot tea ingredient to ease stress.

Pests: aphids, mealybugs, whiteflies

Mint
Mentha spp.

Chocolate mint

If one wanted to tell completely all the virtues, species, and names of mint, one would have to be able to say how many fishes swim in the Red Sea or the number of sparks Vulcan can count flying from the vast furnaces of Etna. **—Walahfrid Strabo, German Abbot, Hortulus, 850–900**

Native to the Middle East, mint is so universally esteemed, introduced varieties are now found growing around the world. Mints belong to the family *Lamiaceae*, which includes the basils, oreganos, rosemaries, sages, thymes, and many other familiar herbs. A large group of delightful aromatic perennial plants in the genus *Mentha*, mints are characterized by their rambling growth habits,

square stems, and a wide assortment of fragrances.

There are countless mint varieties, and like many other herbs, their botanical nomenclature gets somewhat confusing. Mint hybridizes readily and its hybrids tend to revert to other forms. Even nursery catalogs often inaccurately name the mints they offer for sale. Most herb lovers agree the best way to select a good plant is by the nose rather than by the name.

According to Greek mythology, mint acquired its name from a Naiad nymph named Minthe. She was loved by Hades, the god of the Underworld, whose jealous wife, Persephone, turned her into a mint plant, in which form she remains to this day. As mint signifies "find a spouse of your own age and background" in the language of flowers, perhaps this metamorphosis was a means of deliverance from unwelcome attentions.

The Romans believed eating mint would increase intelligence and stop a person from losing their temper. In the Middle Ages, it was used as a strewing herb to keep rooms fresh and to repel mice and rats. Tabletops rubbed with mint leaves symbolized hospitality. Roman naturalist Pliny the Elder held mint in the highest esteem for its many medicinal virtues and remarked, "The very smell of it reanimates the spirit." It was used to whiten teeth, stop hiccups, provide an antidote for the stings of sea serpents or mad dogs, and prevent milk from curdling. And that's not all—if consumed just before an oration, mint will clear the head and voice.

Recent research suggests that sniffing mint may improve your concentration and some international companies pipe minute amounts of mint oil through their air-circulation systems to increase employee productivity. At one time, a bundle of mint hanging near the entrance door was a host's way to welcome guests into the home.

Mints are one of the easiest herbs to grow indoors and are loosely divided into two groups according to fragrance: the spearmints (*M. spicata*) and the peppermints (*M. piperita*). There are countless varieties of mint and they run the gamut of intriguing flavors and cultural requirements.

Orange mint

20 cm) tall and 12 inches (30 cm) or so wide. Treasured for its very special fragrance, this is one of the most delightful and decorative plants you could have in your indoor garden. Its citrusy flavor and scent are tantalizing in fruit punches, teas, and potpourris. A handful of fresh leaves added to warm bath water is like a trip to the spa.

Chocolate Mint
M. × piperita

A popular peppermint cultivar, chocolate mint features dark-green oval leaves with cocoa-colored highlights held on purple stems. Indoors, the plant will reach 10 to 12 inches (23 to 30 cm) in height and at least as wide. Chocolate mint's aroma and flavor are open to interpretation. Some people compare its taste to peppermint candy with chocolate undertones, whereas others discern

■ **POPULAR VARIETIES**

Orange Mint
M. *aquatica* 'Citrata' Bergamot Mint

This variety of mint is sometimes sold as 'Bergamot', 'Orange', or 'Eau de Cologne'.

The fragrance of this plant is a pleasing combination of orange, bergamot, and the sweet scent of basil. It has a dark stem and its rounded, broad leaves are dark green with a lovely tinge of purple. Indoors it reaches 6 to 8 inches (15 to no chocolate flavor whatsoever. Herb expert and flavor artist Susan Belsinger writes in her book, *The Culinary Herbal*, that it has no chocolate flavor but does have a sharp coolness one might associate with chocolate; in other words, the chocolate scent is imaginary. It has a rich, wonderful peppermint flavor and scent and grows well indoors. Use chocolate mint leaves to flavor baked goods, salads, and vinegars. The leaves, fresh or dried, make superb herbal tea for colds. Chocolate mint is an excellent palate cleanser and after-dinner digestion aid.

Pineapple Mint
M. suaveolens 'Variegata'

This decorative cultivar of apple mint has fuzzy puckered oval variegated green- and cream-colored leaves with a sweet fruity pineapple scent. Indoors, the plant will reach 10 to 12 inches (23 to 30 cm) in height and at least as wide. Pineapple mint's trailing growth habit and striking ornamental foliage make it well suited to hanging baskets or left to spill over the edges of an indoor container garden. It is used to flavor tea, jelly, and fruit salads. The trailing leaf stems are beautiful in fresh bouquets or to garnish food and drinks. The dried leaves are often used for color and fragrance in potpourri.

■ LIVING WITH MINT

Common names: mint; assorted varieties often named after their scent

Floral language: eternal refreshment, virtue; "Find a spouse of your own age and background."

Description: Mentha is a genus of square-stemmed, highly aromatic, herbaceous perennials with a spreading growth habit. The leaves may be rounded, oval, or slightly pointed. They can be smooth or wrinkly with slightly toothed or serrated edges, depending on the species. Indoor height is limited by container size and pruning.

Growing conditions: Give mint room to grow. Plant it in a pot at least 12 inches (30 cm) across and 6 to 8 inches (15 to 20 cm) deep in a rapid-draining soil-based potting mix. Moderate to bright light is ideal for this herb. Keep the plant pruned to fit the available space. Mints likes frequent and consistent moisture.

Propagation: Mint is easily propagated by division and cuttings readily root in water. It is a great pass-along houseplant. It's attractive and very useful.

Plant parts used: leaves and flowers

Harvesting & preserving: Mint leaves are used fresh or dried. Pick individual leaves from stems, or harvest entire stems using sharp scissors. Use fresh leaves within a few hours or store whole dried leaves in jars.

Pests: vulnerable to aphids, spider mites, whiteflies

Pineapple mint

The savor or smell of the water minte rejoyceth the heart of man; for which cause they use to strew it in chambers and places of recreation, pleasure, and repose, and where feasts and banquets are made. —**John Gerard,** *The Herball*

THINK MINT!

Mints have a long and colorful history, and they are one genus of herbs whose past uses continue in one form or another in present day. Mint is antibacterial, antiviral, and is used in many bath and body products for soothing itching skin. The many variations available of each of these two simple recipes are testimony to mint's timeless appeal.

Mint Skin Toner

In a medium-size saucepan over medium-low heat, simmer ½ cup (48 g) fresh orange mint or peppermint leaves in 3 cups (720 ml) distilled water for 10 minutes. Let cool and strain the liquid. In a quart-size (960 ml) glass container with a lid, combine the mint infusion with ½ cup (120 ml) organic apple cider vinegar. Keep refrigerated. Use as a skin toner or hair rinse.

Mint Bubble Bath

In a medium-size saucepan over medium-low heat, simmer 1 cup (96 g) fresh mint leaves, 1 cup (96 g) fresh lemon balm leaves, and 3 cups (720 ml) distilled water for 10 minutes. Let cool and strain the liquid. In a quart-size (906 ml) bottle with a lid, combine the herbal infusion and 1 cup (240 ml) liquid soap. Use ¼ cup (60 ml) per bath. This is a fun project for kids to make and use.

Basil

Ocimum spp.

Madonna, wherefore hast thou sent
to me Sweet-basil and mignonette?
Embleming love and health, which
never yet in the same wreath might be.
—**Percy Bysshe Shelley, "To Emilia Viviani"**

Basil is considered the king of fragrant
herbs. A member of the *Lamiaceae* family, basil originates from areas of Asia,
Africa, and Central and South America.
Today this versatile herb is found growing in gardens around the world in all
its colorful and diverse varieties—from
the large lettuce-leaf type to the dwarf
Greek basil with leaves less than 1 inch

(2.5 cm) in size. The smell of basil is
"good for the heart and the head." The
fragrance is best described as stimulating, at once spicy, sweet, and clove-like,
with a hint of anise and mint.

Basil is primarily used in cooking but
it is also used for medicinal purposes,
in toiletries, and as an aphrodisiac. Basil
makes a decorative and fragrant addition
to flower arrangements and a pot of basil
on a windowsill is a natural way to discourage flies. Basil was once a courting
herb; however, it was also a symbol of
hate and the Greeks used it to represent

'Genovese'

poverty and disgrace. Despite this controversial history, everyone agrees on its lovely fragrance. Basil comes in a bedazzling range of flavors and fragrances and new varieties appear annually. Some do better than others growing indoors.

■ POPULAR VARIETIES
Sweet basil, also known as 'Genovese,' is a voluptuous aromatic variety with smooth, shiny, deep-green leaves. This basil is an indispensable ingredient in Mediterranean-inspired dishes, pestos, and for seasoning fresh tomatoes.

Lemon basil's light green leaves have a lovely lemony aroma and taste, perfect for flavoring iced tea and lemonade.

'Mrihani' is a beautiful basil with ruffled, purple-striped, light-green leaves. Its scent has a sweet floral quality with fennel undertones, and it is resistant to downy mildew.

■ HERBAL LIFE
Chopped green basil and toasted sesame seeds mixed into cream cheese makes a very tasty filling for celery sticks.

'Mrihani'

Lemon Basil

■ LIVING WITH BASIL

Common names: Basil varieties are often named after the plant's scent or physical aspects. Best indoor varieties and cultivars include 'Genovese', Greek, Lemon, and Thai basil.

Floral language: best wishes, hatred

Description: Basil is a tender herb in the genus Ocimum with many species and a great variety of fragrances, leaf shapes, and colors. Grown indoors, these plants range in size from 1 foot (30 cm) to several feet in height.

Growing conditions: Provide as much direct bright sunlight as possible, or use artificial lights to grow basil indoors. Loose, well-draining soil is best. Keep basil plants moist but not constantly wet and provide good ventilation. Pinch out tip shoots to encourage bushy growth and do not permit basil to flower because it will complete its growth cycle and die.

Propagation: Basil is propagated by seed and stem cutting.

Plant parts used: leaves; flowers are also edible

Harvesting & preserving: Pick leaves when young. Use the leaves fresh or dried, freeze them, or infuse them in vinegar. Basil may also be infused in olive oil. Use fresh leaves in salads, vinegar, baked goods, and a variety of cuisines.

Pests: Aphids and whiteflies are common pests. Replace plants annually, or as needed.

Oregano
and Plants Called Oregano
Origanum sp.

> Where the bee can suck no honey, she leaves her sting behind; and where the bear cannot find origanum to heal his grief, he blasts all other leaves with his breath. —**John Lyly, Campaspe and Sappho and Phao, 1580**

The generic name *Origanum* comes from the Greek words "joy of the mountains" and refers to the gay fragrant floral performance these plants give blooming on the hillsides in their native homeland, the Mediterranean. The Romans and Greeks crowned marital couples with marjoram to symbolize love, honor, and happiness and the herb was planted on graves to wish the deceased well in the afterlife.

The oreganos have an ancient history of medicinal and culinary use, along with some very confusing nomenclature. Many plants throughout the world contain the same essential oil that gives oregano its fragrance—they do not look like oregano, but they smell like oregano. Founding member of the International Herb Association, Chuck Voigt, says, "To some extent oregano is a flavor, more than an individual plant." True oregano comes from the genus *Origanum*. But Mexican oregano, *Lippia graveolens*, and Cuban oregano, *Plectranthus amboinicus* also have the scent and flavor known as oregano, although Cuban oregano is not used in cooking.

The "true" oreganos are aromatic square-stemmed herbaceous perennials in the mint family. They vary in their cultural requirements, uses, foliage, and growth habit. Some are grown for their ornamental attributes and aromatic foliage, others for seasoning. Good culinary oregano has a hot peppery flavor and a freshly picked leaf will tingle in your mouth. Plants vary widely in their culinary intensity, so when choosing an oregano, smell it to make sure it has a strong pungent fragrance, then taste a tiny bit of the leaf.

Oregano is a popular herb in a wide variety of cuisines. Greeks, Italians, and Spaniards were the first to use oregano in their cooking; from there the Spaniards introduced it to Mexico. It is a basic herb flavoring in chili powder blends and oregano marries well with strong-flavored foods such as beef, citrus, lamb, and tomatoes. An infusion of oregano tea before an ocean voyage was thought to prevent seasickness.

Greek Oregano
O. vulgare hirtum

Large, dark-green leaves cover the plant's hairy square stems. This oregano variety has a spreading growth habit with white flowers and reaches 12 to 18 inches (30 to 45 cm) tall grown indoors. The leaves have an assertive oregano flavor, and when chewed alone, make the tongue tingle. Most culinary experts agree that this variety, also called Greek oregano, has the best biting, pungent flavor for use in the kitchen.

Variegated Oregano
O. vulgare 'Variegata'

A very ornamental plant with attractive white-yellow variegated leaves and a low, creeping prostrate habit that reaches 6 inches (15 cm) in height. Its flavor is similar to common marjoram. This oregano variety makes a lovely garnish for salads, vegetables, and fruit dishes.

Oregano 'Dwarf'
O. microphyllum

An annual sweet dwarf oregano originating from Crete, this herb is one of the ingredients in Cretan Mountain Tea. Darling tiny aromatic silvery blue-green leaves are held on tough wiry stems on which purple flowers bloom. It reaches 10 to 12 inches (25 to 30 cm) in height. Introduced into the trade by Theresa Mieseler of Shady Acres Herb Farm.

Greek

Sweet Marjoram
O. majorana

A tender perennial, sweet marjoram is a short, erect, shrubby plant with gray-green leaves covered with very fine short hairs held on light purplish stems that reach 10 to 12 inches (25 to 30 cm) in height. When marjoram is ready to flower, it produces little rounded clusters of pale-green bracts that surround the tiny white flowers, which has given it the name *knotted marjoram*. Marjoram has a smoother taste than its relative, oregano. The English used marjoram as a tea before black and green teas were imported from Asia; blended and brewed with savory and rosemary it makes a refreshing herbal iced tea.

Variegated

'Compactum'

Mexican Oregano
Lippia graveolens

Mexican oregano, *L. graveolens*, also known as Puerto Rican oregano, is a member of the verbena family. An upright shrubby plant, it has slightly rough oval green, delicately scalloped leaves and pretty cream-colored flowers. This plant's highly aromatic foliage has a citrusy oregano taste. Given a bright sunny window, this plant adapts well to an indoor environment. It is good in tomato sauce, sautéed vegetables, and marinades.

Sweet Marjoram

The sweetness of marjoram and the spiciness of oregano complement each other well. When cooking with marjoram, add it to the food near the end of the cooking process as the flavor is not as robust as oregano.

■ LIVING WITH OREGANO

Common names: Greek, Italian, and Mexican oregano; knotted marjoram, sweet marjoram

Floral language: happiness, joy

Description: The oreganos are a hardy, slightly woody group of perennials with a creeping root system. Oregano leaves are oval to elliptical in shape with a rich robust aromatic scent. Flowers range from white to light purple. Plants vary from 6 to 18 inches (15 to 45 cm) high; some varieties are erect and others more prostrate in their growth habit.

Growing conditions: Provide loose, well-draining soil and full sunshine. Oreganos must have 5 to 6 hours of direct sunlight daily. The plants are moderately tolerant of dry soil conditions. Water as needed and never let the plant sit in water.

Propagation: Most oreganos do not come true from seed, especially with regard to flavor. They're best propagated by stem tip cuttings or crown divisions.

Plant parts used: leaves, fresh and dried

Harvesting & preserving: Snip off leaves as needed when plants are in full growth. Freeze or dry the leaves, or infuse them in oil or vinegar. Oregano is a vigorous grower and benefits from heavy pruning if the plants get leggy.

Pests: aphids, mealy bugs, spider mites; plant diseases include root rot and powdery mildew

Mexican oregano

Parsley
Petroselinum crispum

Flat leaf

Curled

> Parsley is the crown of cookery. It once crowned man; it now crowns his food. —**Irma Goodrich Mazza, Herbs for the Kitchen**

Native to Southern Europe and the Eastern Mediterranean, a friendly, humble herb, parsley has a fascinating and bewildering past.

Parsley was one of the first plants used in wreath-making. The ancient Greeks wore chaplets of parsley at banquets to absorb the fumes of wine to delay inebriation. They crowned their victorious athletes with parsley wreaths and festooned the graves of loved ones with parsley garlands. As parsley took root and flourished at burial sites, it came to be associated with death, the Underworld, and ill-fortune. Because parsley is slow to germinate and difficult to transplant, legend has it that parsley seed goes to the devil seven times before it will sprout. In keeping with parsley's baffling history, other plant lore links this herb with life and joy. An old English nursery rhyme dating to the seventeenth century tells us, "Babies come from parsley beds."

As the green sprig delicately garnishing entrées or side dishes, parsley is probably one of the most familiar culinary herbs. There is simply no end to the kitchen uses of this versatile herb. It has a pleasant delicate taste of its own and the happy capacity to enhance the flavor of more dominant herbs. Parsley is rich in minerals, chlorophyll, and vitamins A and C.

There are two kinds of parsley suitable for indoor culture. Curly parsley (*P. crispum*), with tightly curled fringed leaves arranged in bright green clumps on short, sturdy stems, is used more as a garnish. In contrast, flat-leaf, or Italian, parsley (*P. crispum neapolitanum*) has flat, dark-green glossy green leaves resembling cilantro and a more pronounced flavor—the good cook's choice.

■ HERBAL LIFE
Eat your garnish! Parsley contains lots of chlorophyll; it is a healthful natural breath freshener.

■ LIVING WITH PARSLEY
Common names: curly, flat-leaf, French, Italian, plain

Floral language: festivity, joy, victory; "The woman of the house is boss."

Description: Parsley is a biennial herb that grows from a long taproot and reaches to 1½ feet (45 cm) tall and 1 foot (30 cm) wide.

Growing conditions: Parsley is an excellent herb for growing in containers. Space plants 6 to 8 inches (15 to 20 cm)

apart. Parsley is short-lived, so you'll need to replace plants annually, or as needed. Provide bright light either from direct sunlight or an artificial grow light. Evenly moist soil conditions are best.

Propagation: Plant parsley seeds directly into pots.

Plant parts used: Leaves, fresh or dried, or freeze for later use

Harvesting & preserving: Snip off parsley leaves as needed, using the older outer leaves first. Use it generously in soups, salads, herb butters, vinegar, and salts. It makes a delicious addition to green drinks.

Pests: aphids, mealybugs, whiteflies

Rosemary

Rosmarinus officinalis

As for Rosemary, I let it run all over my garden walls, not only because my bees love it, but because it is the herb sacred to remembrance and friendship.
—Thomas More

A member of the mint family, rosemary is a small perennial evergreen shrub native to the Mediterranean region's rocky cliffs. The picturesque sight of the sunlight twinkling on the plant's flowers and leaves drenched with morning dew earned rosemary the charming nickname "dew of the sea." It has been said that if basil is the king of herbs, rosemary must be the queen. For more than 2,000 years, this versatile herb has been treasured for its heady aroma, medicinal virtues, and gourmet delights. In folklore, rosemary is a symbol of fidelity associated with remembrance, friendship, and love, and it is traditionally used at weddings and funerals. *Incensier* is an old French term for rosemary, as it was used for that purpose in churches and cathedrals to purify and disinfect the air.

According to ancient lore, rosemary sprigs placed under pillows or hung in doorways had the power to keep witches at bay and ward off bad dreams. Rosemary wreaths were worn at one time by students to stimulate the memory during exams and recent studies with aromatherapy appear to confirm this benefit. In the fourteenth century, Queen Isabella of Hungary claimed that using Hungary water (rosemary leaves macerated in white wine) so restored her health and beauty at the age of 72 that the king of Poland proposed to her. British herbalist and author of *Modern Herbal* (1931), Maude Grieve, notes that rosemary was a traditional New Year's gift in England

Rosemary is a popular herb with people who like to grow topiaries. The upright varieties are a natural for training as standards and the prostrate varieties' flexible branches can be shaped into intricate heart or circle shapes. Pine-scented rosemary is a wonderful addition to potpourri.

There are many popular rosemary varieties to choose from and forms range from upright to trailing. The plant's needlelike leaves range in color from soft gray-green to deep forest green. Some species bear shiny broad, or very narrow, foliage showing gray or white undersides, with blossoms of light rose, pale lavender, or pale to dark blue. Rosemary's spicy leaf scent may be camphorous, piney, resinous, or even lemony. When selecting a rosemary for indoor culture look for plant types that do well in pots.

Tuscan Blue Rosemary
R. o. **'Tuscan Blue'**
This rosemary variety is prized for its ornamental attributes, pine scent, and smooth textured grayish-green needles. It has a fabulous upright robust columnar shape with thick stems, succulent fat leaves, and large clear-blue flowers. Its flavor and aroma are a little milder than some of other rosemaries and it is a favorite of chefs. Excellent variety for topiary training.

Blue Boy Rosemary
R. o. **'Blue Boy'**
Blue Boy rosemary is a dwarf, or miniature, cultivar that is a natural for pots and a perfect choice for where common-size rosemaries would be too large. A tidy compact slow-growing plant, offering a profusion of long-blooming light-blue flowers held over small evergreen leaves. Unique for its small size, just 6 to 10 inches (15 to 25 cm) high, it's a charming little rosemary for an indoor fairy garden and it tastes great, too.

'Blue Boy'

'Tuscan Blue'

'Shady Acres'

Shady Acres

R. o. 'Shady Acres'

Developed in Minnesota on Shady Acres Herb Farm by Theresa Mieseler, this is a prime-choice culinary rosemary, exceptional for its flavor and form. It is a fast grower with a strong upright form and dark-green leaves.

■ HERBAL LIFE

Rosemary marries well with orange. Use it to flavor orange jelly, or use it chopped fresh on orange slices or citrus salad. Use rosemary to season cranberry juice and add it to cranberry jelly.

■ LIVING WITH ROSEMARY

Common names: rosemary

Floral language: fidelity, friendship, loyalty

Description: Commonly grown rosemaries are almost all selections from the species *Rosmarinus officinalis*. Plant types vary from strictly upright to pendent, with some intermediate shapes. The leaves are stemless, needlelike, and fragrant. The blossoms may be white-rose, pale lavender, or dark blue and will start to bloom indoors in late winter.

Growing conditions: Provide bright light, including direct sunlight. Rosemary plants are finicky about how they are watered. Always provide good drainage. Never allow soil to dry out completely and reduce watering in winter. Placing rosemary on trays of pebbles, which are kept moist, helps counteract low humidity situations. Prune after flowering and replace plants as needed.

Propagation: Rosemary is propagated by seed and stem cutting. Seed propagation is slow and undependable.

Plant parts used: leaves, fresh or dried

Harvesting & preserving: Cut bunches of the leaf-covered stems and hang them to dry. Strip the leaves from the dry brittle stems and store in a sealed glass jar. Use in culinary application, medicines, teas, bath and body preparations, sauces, and jelly.

Pests: whiteflies; plant disease powdery mildew

Bloody Dock

Rumex sanguineus

Sorrel sharpens the appetite, assuages heat, cools the liver, and strengthens the heart . . .

And in the making of sallets imparts a grateful quickness to the rest as supplying the want of oranges and lemons. Together with salt, it gives both the name and the relish to sallets from the sapidity, which renders not plants and herbs only, but men themselves pleasant and agreeable.

—John Evelyn, 1720

Sorrel is native to Europe, Southwest Asia, and Northern Africa. Generally, sorrels are related to the docks but are much more palatable than their wild weedy relatives. Both sorrels and docks belong to genus *Rumex*, a Latin word alluding to the lance-shaped leaves. This leafy green is grown for its tart lemony flavor and the most commonly cultivated sorrel is the broad-leafed French sorrel (*Rumex scutatus*) and narrow-leafed garden sorrel (*R. acetosa*). Less familiar, bloody dock or red-veined sorrel (*R. sanguineus*), is valued for its colorful ornamental foliage; its light green lance-shaped leaves are vividly veined purple to red.

Irish peasants regularly served sorrel leaves with fish and milk dishes to prevent scurvy. Some religious scholars believe St. Patrick used sorrel leaves, not clover, to illustrate the Holy Trinity, and consider sorrel to be the first shamrock. According to ancient Chinese folklore, the juice from sorrel leaves is an effective remedy to remove freckles.

Red sorrel leaves make a very colorful and tasty addition to fresh salads and sharpen the flavor of the greens with a lively hint of citrus. Historically, sorrel was used to treat cancer and various blood diseases.

■ **HERBAL LIFE**

Sorrel is an acidic herb and its sourness is welcome to the palate when mixed with other greens.

■ **LIVING WITH BLOODY DOCK**

Common names: bloodwort, red-veined sorrel

Floral language: patience

Description: Bloody dock is an ornamental tap-rooted rosette-forming perennial plant with striking 3- to 6-inch (7.5 to 15 cm) light green, lance-shaped leaves marked with bright maroon-colored veins. Indoors, sorrel reaches 12 inches (30 cm) tall and grows 6 to 10 inches (15 to 25 cm) wide.

Growing conditions: For optimum growth, provide bright light, including direct sunlight, and keep the soil evenly moist. Grow indoors year-round in cool temperatures. To maintain good growth, pinch flower stalks as they appear.

Propagation: Propagate sorrel by seed or root divisions.

Plant parts used: Fresh leaves are best harvested when young; older leaves are bitter and tough.

Harvesting & preserving: Red sorrel leaves lend a fresh lemony tang to fresh salads and citrus fruit dishes. Cut young leaves from the center of the plant as they develop, using a pair of pruners or sharp scissors.

Pests: relatively pest free; occasional issues with whiteflies, spider mites, and aphids

Sage
Salvia officinalis

The "herb of longevity," sage has been highly regarded as a medicinal plant since ancient times. The plant's specific epithet, *officinalis*, means "of the shops," or medicinal. A perennial plant native to the northern shores of the Mediterranean, sage is one of the herbs still universally used for flavoring food. The name *salvia*, from the Latin *salvere*, to be in good health, to cure, to save, aptly reflects this herb's charitable nature. In the Middle Ages it was used as a cure-all, rather like people use aspirin today.

Growing sage is said to prolong life and another old folk tradition says sage only prospers where the wife rules the house. In French, sage means *wise* and regular use of sage tea was supposed to restore the memory as well as banish melancholy and depression. The English introduced sage tea to the Chinese, who would exchange four pounds of tea for one pound of sage. They used it in preference to their teas to relieve headaches. The accent Egyptians used sage to increase fertility.

Garden sage is the most commonly known of the eight hundred or so species of this very large genus in the mint family. An entire book could be devoted to salvias; for windowsill use, it's a great one to start with.

> Sage is singularly good for the head and brain; it quickeneth the senses and the memory; strengthens the sinews; restores health to those that have palsy; and takes away tremblings of the members.
> **—John Gerard, English herbalist, 1649**

■ HERBAL LIFE

Dried sage or thyme is great in corn-meal muffins or as a cornmeal meat pie topping. Also, a handful of finely minced sage in biscuit dough for a stew is great. Alternatively, try this: Using your favorite biscuit recipe, roll out the dough, spread it with room-temperature butter, sprinkle with crumbled sage, garlic salt, chopped fresh parsley, and a little grated cheese to taste. Roll the dough, cut into biscuits, and bake according to the recipe instructions.

■ LIVING WITH SAGE

Common names: garden sage, sage, salvia

Floral language: domestic virtues; long life and good health; "I will suffer all for you."

Description: Sage is a shrubby strongly aromatic herb with pebbly, soft, oblong gray-green leaves held on stiff stems that become woody with age. Culinary sage may have spikes of blue, pink, white, or blue flowers in summer. Sage reaches 1 to 1½ feet (30 to 45 cm) tall when grown as a houseplant indoors.

Growing conditions: Place potted sage in a south-facing window with bright light, including direct sunlight. Sage is moderately tolerant of dry soil conditions. Water only as needed and never let the plant sit in water. Cut back the stems after flowering. Be sure to water plants directly on the soil. Water on the foliage will lead to mold.

Propagation: best propagated by seed and stem cuttings

Plant parts used: leaves, fresh or dried

Harvesting & preserving: Harvest fresh leaves as needed. Hang bunches to dry or place them on a drying screen. Harvest often and dry, freeze, or infuse the harvested leaves in vinegar or olive oil. Use in teas, herbal butters, and vegetable dishes. Sage is also useful as a medicinal. The leaves are attractive in wreathes and bouquets.

Pests: aphids, spider mites

Salad Burnet

Sanguisorba minor

Salad burnet is native to Europe and Asia, and curiously enough, it is a member of the rose family, *Rosaceae*. The genus name *Sanguisorba minor* comes from the Latin *sangus*, "blood," and *sobere*, "to stop." Salad burnet has a styptic quality and was used long ago to stanch the flow of blood. In Hungary, it is called Chabairje (Chaba's salve); according to legend, its virtues were discovered by King Chaba after engaging in a terrible battle with his brother. He is said to have healed the wounds of fifteen thousand soldiers with the juice of burnet. Salad burnet was one of the first herbs brought to America by the colonists. It was believed to protect against infections and reduce the risk of gout if mixed in wine or beer.

But those which perfume the air most delightfully, not passed by as the rest, but being trodden upon and crushed, are three: That is Burnet, Wilde-Time, and Water-Mints. Therefore, you are to set whole allies of them, to have the pleasure, when you walk or tread.

—Francis Bacon, *An Essay of Gardens*, 1625

Renowned houseplant expert Tovah Martin writes in her book *The Unexpected House Plant*, "Although not in the mainstream with the herbal superstars such as parsley, sage, rosemary, and thyme, salad burnet is windowsill worthy." It looks a bit like a small compact fern growing in a pot indoors.

■ **HERBAL LIFE**

Salad burnet is more than pretty. The plant's trailing dark-green leaves have a subtle cucumberlike taste. And, as its name suggests, the leaves make a wonderful addition to a salad.

■ **LIVING WITH SALAD BURNET**

Common names: burnet, salad burnet

Floral language: a merry heart; joy

Description: Salad burnet is a short-lived herbaceous perennial. It has a lovely circular clumping growth habit and elegant wispy, daintily serrated dark-green leaves. Potted plants reach 8 to 12 inches (20 to 30 cm) in height and 6 to 12 inches (15 to 30 cm) wide.

Growing conditions: Provide bright light, including direct sunlight. Salad burnet is moderately tolerant of dry soil conditions. Water only as needed and never let the plant sit in water.

Propagation: easily propagated by seed

Plant parts used: fresh leaves

Harvesting & preserving: Use the leaves in salads and for flavoring vinegars, cream cheese, green sauces, and garnishing.

Pests: aphids, spider mites

Savory

Satureja spp.

Savory is an aromatic genus in the mint family (*Lamiaceae*), native to southern Europe and the eastern Mediterranean. The origin of the genus name *Satureja*, is said to stem from the Latin *satyr*, or the Middle Eastern spice *za'atar*, or the from the Hebrew *sathra*—botanists are still arguing over the name origin to this day. The only thing we know for sure: Savory is still valued and popular the world over. The German name for savory is *bohnenkraut*, or "bean herb," because it enhances the flavor of beans and aids digestion.

Summer savory and winter savory are used basically the same way in culinary dishes. On the other hand, winter and summer savory were believed to affect sex drive in opposite ways. Winter savory is thought to decrease sex drive, whereas summer savory will increase the libido. According to Greek mythology, the satyrs lived in meadows of savory, hinting it was the herb that made them passionate.

Savory has an appealing taste, similar to oregano and thyme. This quality makes it friendly with many herbs and, perhaps, the reason savory has been included in kitchen gardens for medicinal and culinary use for thousands of years.

Mercury claims dominion over this herb, neither is there a better remedy against the colic and iliac passion, than this herb; keep it dry by you all the year, if you love yourself and your ease . . .
—Nicholas Culpepper, *Complete Herbal,* **1653**

■ HERBAL LIFE

This herb comes in two different forms—summer savory (*Satureja hortensis*), an annual plant with narrow green leaves and an erect growth habit, and winter savory (*S. montana*), a shrubby perennial with small glossy dark aromatic green leaves. Lemon savory (*S. biflora*) is a perennial native to South Africa and has the same growth habit and requirements as winter savory, but its leaves have a bright lemony flavor and fragrance.

■ LIVING WITH SAVORY

Common names: lemon savory, summer savory, winter savory

Floral language: interest, mental powers, "the truth may be bitter"

Description: Summer savory and winter savory have many of the same properties. Summer savory is the preferred savory for culinary purposes; winter savory has a more pungent and biting flavor and grows better indoors. Savory is a sprawling plant indoors and averages 8 to 12 inches (20 to 30 cm) tall.

Growing conditions: Provide bright light, including direct sunlight, and loose well-drained soil. Savory is moderately tolerant of dry soil conditions, so water only when needed.

Never let the base of the pot sit in water. To promote growth, prune the plant regularly. Try one of each variety.

Propagation: Savoy is easily propagated from root divisions, cuttings, or seed.

Plant parts used: leaves

Harvesting & preserving: Harvest often to generate new growth. Dry, freeze, or infuse the leaves in vinegar or olive oil. Use in teas, herbal butters, and vegetable dishes.

Pests: aphids, spider mites

Stevia
Stevia rebaudiana

For he who rightly cares for his own eating, will not be a bad cook. And if you keep your organs, sense, and taste, in proper order, you will not err. But often taste your dishes while you are boiling them. Do they want salt? Add some; is any other reasoning needed? Add it, and taste again, till you have arrived at harmony of flavour; like man, who highly tunes a lyre till it rightly sounds . . . Bring in a troop of willing damsels fair, equal in number to the banqueters.
—Athenaeus, *The Deipnosophists, or Banquet of the Learned of Athenaeus*

Stevia is a tender perennial shrub native to Paraguay and it is a member of the *Asteraceae* family. It has been used for over 1,500 years by native Central and South American peoples as a sweetener, digestive aid, and topical healing agent. Stevia was first raised commercially in Japan in the1970s and Japan presently remains the largest producer and consumer of stevia, using it as a sweetener for pickles, dried seafood, soy sauce, and bean paste. In North America, stevia is employed as a natural sweetener. Stevia plants vary in their sweetness level. Organic gardeners are experimenting with stevia due to its reputed insect-repelling properties.

■ HERBAL LIFE

A short-lived plant, stevia has earned the reputation of being finicky. Plant this herb alone; it requires more water and sunlight and has been known to go dormant and drop its leaves in winter.

■ LIVING WITH STEVIA

Common names: honey leaf, sugar leaf, sweet herb

Floral language: divine beneficence

Description: Stevia is a shrubby tender perennial with a tall upright growth habit with moderately broad green leaves. It reaches about 2 feet (60 cm) high at maturity. White tubular flowers with light-purple accents are borne in terminal clusters.

Growing conditions: A sunny window is perfect for stevia. Provide bright light, including direct sunlight. If your plant is not growing well, add artificial light. Keep the soil evenly moist but good drainage is a must. Never allow the soil to dry out completely and reduce waterings in winter. Prune the plant regularly to promote a bushier shape and encourage a better branching plant. This plant is short-lived; replace plants annually, or as needed.

Propagation: by seed or root cutting

Plant parts used: leaves

Harvesting & preserving: Snip leaves, as needed, when plants are in full growth; the best-quality leaves occur before flowering. Stevia leaves can be used fresh, infused to sweeten tea and other beverages, and in some baking recipes. When buds appear, harvest the whole plant by cutting it off at the base and hang it to dry.

Pests: aphids

Thyme
Thymus vulgaris

Variegated thyme

I know a bank whereon the wild thyme blows, where oxlips and nodding violets grows; Quite overcanopied with luscious woodbine, with sweet musk roses and eglantine. **—William Shakespeare, *A Midsummer Night's Dream***

Fair and fragrant thyme is perhaps the most useful and used of all culinary herbs. A friendly, congenial plant, thyme is one of the oldest-recorded culinary herbs and is included in a wide array of international ingredients and recipes. Through the centuries, thyme has also had innumerable medical uses.

The genus name for thyme was derived from several Greek words: *thymon*, meaning to fumigate, and *thymus*, which signified courage, as its properties were supposed to instill courage. It was also a symbol of graceful elegance. "To smell of thyme" was an expression of praise.

Not only an emblem of bravery, thyme was also an emblem of energy and activity and it was the custom of ladies of medieval times to embroider a bee hovering over a sprig of thyme on the scarves they presented to their knights to ensure success in battle.

Old tradition tells us that thyme was part of the "manger herbs" of the Virgin Mary and the Christ Child. Thyme, sage, lavender, rosemary, and juniper are traditional herbs associated with the Christmas holiday season.

The thymes belong to a large genus with three hundred or so species distributed throughout Eurasia. There are basically two main groups: the upright shrubby types like cooking or common thyme, *Thymus vulgaris* and the ground-hugging varieties such as creeping thyme, *T. serpyllum*. According to Rex Talbert, nationally respected expert on thymes, the most useful culinary thymes are French, lemon, caraway, and oregano thyme. These thymes are also very suited for indoor culture.

English or French Thyme
T. vulgaris
Cooking thyme has an upright shrubby growth habit with twiggy stems rising from a woody base and a huge assortment of growth habits, leaf sizes, colors, and scents. English or winter thyme is the hardiest and most popular cooking thyme whereas French or summer thyme has finer gray-green leaves, tastes sweeter, and is less robust than English thyme. Either one is great with tomato-based dishes, pizzas, focaccia, and fresh vegetables.

Silver Posie Thyme
***T. v.* 'Argenteus'**
A spectacular variegated upright thyme with pretty white-edged gray-green leaves. The tips of the foliage take on a pink hue when located in a room with cooler temperatures. This plant reaches 6 to 12 inches (15 to 30 cm) tall and 9 to 12 inches (22.5 to 30 cm) wide. It is an excellent culinary herb—the leaves have a savory taste and pleasing fragrance. A very decorative container plant, it makes a great temporary botanical accent plant for a special occasion.

Lemon thyme

Lemon Thyme
T. × citriodora
A spreading subshrub, lemon thyme has a mounding habit and reaches 8 to 10 inches (20 to 25 cm) tall growing indoors. This rapidly growing thyme has deep-green leaves imbued with a sweet lemony fragrance. The growth habit of this plant makes it a perfect choice for a hanging basket in a kitchen window, keeping it close at hand for daily culinary use. Lemon thyme is a natural for fish, poultry, and desserts and it makes a delightful syrup or vinegar and a lovely lemony herbal tea.

■ **HERBAL LIFE**

Thyme's affinity to blend flavors is not limited to cooked food, it is also great in hot and cold teas. Its spicy quality not only enhances herbal blends, it's also perfect on its own. Thyme tea is used to relieve coughs and congestion.

■ **LIVING WITH THYME**

Common names: cooking thyme, English, French, upright thyme

Floral language: courage, happiness, thriftiness

Description: There are many varieties of thyme, each with a different growth habit. Whether upright or prostrate, thyme has tiny leaves that range in color from glossy dark green to silver or variegated green. Leaves are held on wiry stems. Minute starlike flowers in shades of pink and white appear in summer. Indoors, thyme grows to various heights, but usually not more than 6 to 10 inches (15 to 25 cm).

Growing conditions: Thyme needs south-facing windows and 5 to 6 hours of direct sunlight daily. Additional artificial light is sometimes needed. Provide loose, well-draining soil; thyme is moderately tolerant of dry soil conditions; water as needed and never let the plant sit in water. Improper watering could lead to fungal diseases such as gray mold and root rot.

Propagation: seed, divisions, or cuttings

Plant parts used: leaves and flowers

Harvesting & preserving: Snip leaves as needed when plants are in full growth. Thyme is easily dried by hanging the stems or placing them on screens. Use the leaves fresh or dried in cooking, medicine, crafts, and for ornamental purposes.

Pests: fungus gnats

3.
Herbs for
Fun and Fragrance

Smells and other odours are sweeter in the air at some distance, than near the nose . . . For we see that in sounds likewise, they are sweetest when we cannot hear every part by itself.
—Francis Bacon

The sense of smell is one of Mother Nature's most precious gifts and fragrance is one of life's greatest pleasures. The restorative comfort and healing power of fragrance touches everyone. In her charming book *The Fragrant Garden*, Louise Beebe Wilder describes the evocative power of scent, "It is born of sensitive and very personal preferences yet its appeal is almost universal. Fragrance speaks to many whom color and form say little, and it can bring as irresistibly as music emotions of all sorts to the mind."

Botanical scents can be potent medicines as well as pleasant perfumes. Aromatherapy's power comes from its ability to effect changes in both mood and health. If you have ever smelled pine and felt more energetic or if a particular fragrance brings back memories of a loved one, then you have experienced the influence of scent on your psychological state. Research has documented this link, confirming that scent is an important factor in mental performance, memory, and mood.

HERBAL HOUSEPLANTS JUST FOR FUN

If you don't get an imagination as a child, you probably never will. **—Dr. Seuss**

Both indoor and outdoor gardening develop two distinct kinds of plant enthusiasts. If it takes more than just a pretty herb for flavor or fragrance to arouse the gardening impulse, perhaps some of the plants described here just for fun will do the trick.

A large portion of houseplants sold today originate from South Africa. Given the diverse and varying climatic conditions in South Africa, the plants from this part of the world are tough and adaptable, making them no-fuss indoor houseplants. Sansevieria, wild banana, zebra plant, and aloe vera are just a few of the green emigrants that have traveled across the vast seas and around the world to accent homes. The following plants also origi-nate from South Africa and are not only lovely ornamental houseplants but also delightful conversation pieces.

Sea Onion
Ornithogalum caudatum

The sea onion is native to South Africa and tropical East Africa and is a member of the lily family. A whimsical, charming plant specimen, it is one of the easiest houseplants to grow. The sea onion is an old-fashioned pass-along plant and it was very popular with indoor gardeners back in the 1940s and '50s. The plant is reputed to have healing effects similar to aloe vera.

This plant is not an onion but it sure does resemble one. Pregnant onion and false sea onion are other common names. It is classic *cryptophyte*, a plant with a bulb-stem that goes dormant during the hot, dry months.

The plant's bulb, a pale opalescent-green onionlike object, grows in a pot

three-quarters out of the soil. From the top, 1-inch (2.5 cm)-wide, semisucculent glossy ribbonlike leaves rise like a fountain and tumble downward. If you cut them short, they curl into ringlets, or you can let them grow long and trail. Spectacular blossoms form on a long raceme—a sheath of white starry fragrant flowers.

The bulb is composed of numerous layers of skin and, between these layers, little bulblets, or litters, form. At first they look like swellings on the side of the bulb and eventually ripen and fall from the parent plant. Repot the yearlings or bulblets and pass along to friends. This plant is very tolerant of neglect and will only die if overwatered.

African Power Cress
Spilanthes filicaulis

Spilanthes is a genus originating in tropical Africa and South America and belongs to the *Asteraceae* family. These plants have been cultivated for thousands of years for horticultural, medicinal, insecticidal, and culinary purposes. African power cress is a low creeping variety and makes a very ornamental houseplant for a hanging basket or pot.

The plant's leaves and pretty yellow button flowers produce a lemony tingling sensation on the tongue, due to spilantho, a mild analgesic property found in other *Spilanthes* species. According to Canadian herb expert Conrad Richter, top chefs worldwide are experimenting with *Spilanthes* cresses in salads for an "electric" tingling effect. Richter encourages people to try a few chopped leaves or flowers in a salad mix and see what happens. In West Africa, this plant is said to increase the powers of persuasion and influence.

Chewing the plant's fresh flowers or leaves will make one's speech smooth and harmonious and local leaders are known to use it before high-priority meetings and public gatherings. A great plant for a workplace to help increase your power to influence co-workers and management.

Supply bright light, including direct sunlight, and keep the soil evenly moist. This plant is susceptible to spider mites.

Cardamom

Elettaria cardamomum

> Herbs do comfort the wearied brain with fragrant smells which yield a certain kind of nourishment.
> —**William Coles, *The Art of Simpling*, 1656**

Cardamom is a closely related member of the ginger family, native to southern India. Cardamom's botanical name comes from the Sanskrit *ela*, referring to the plant's green, distinctively pungent, warmly aromatic seeds. The plant's well-documented history of use in Ayurvedic medicine can be traced back to the fourth century BCE. Indians call the plant's fragrant seeds the "queen of spices"; following saffron and vanilla,

cardamom seeds are the third most expensive spice in the world.

In its native habitat, cardamom is a perennial shrub and may grow to 10 feet (300 cm), but when grown as a houseplant, depending on the warmth and humidity of the environment, it seldom reaches more than 2½ feet (75 cm) tall. A majestic plant, its alternately spaced, lance-shaped leaves are dark green with pale undersides covered with soft silky hairs. Cardamom rarely flowers or sets seed indoors; even so, it makes a fabulous indoor evergreen plant. What could be lovelier than a houseplant that gives off an aromatic, clean, refreshing scent when you brush its leaves?

Commercially, the cardamom essential oil is processed from the plant's seeds and is used to flavor bitters and liqueurs and to scent perfumes. In the Middle East, cardamom is used to flavor sweets and coffee; in Scandinavia it is used to flavor stewed fruits, meatballs, and traditional breads, cookies, and pancakes. In India, cardamom is part of a mixture of chewing-spices consumed as an after-dinner ritual to aid digestion and clear the palette. Historically, the seeds were an ingredient in love potions, or chewed as a breath freshener to encourage a potential lover.

■ HERBAL LIFE

Tuck a few fragrant cardamom leaves in your pillowcase at night and wake in the morning rested and refreshed.

■ LIVING WITH CARDAMOM

Common names: ela, grains of paradise, queen of spices

Floral language: peaceful thoughts

Description: Cardamom is a vigorous-growing, tender perennial plant. An attractive tropical foliage plant with a pleasing cinnamon-cardamom fragrance. It reaches an average height of 2 feet (60 cm) tall and 2 feet (60 cm) wide.

Growing conditions: Cardamom likes rich, evenly moist soil and bright, but indirect, sunlight. A rhizomatous plant, cut it back and repot it each year in spring.

Propagation: Divide rhizomes to increase the number of plants. Seed germination is poor and irregular.

Plant parts used: fresh leaves

Harvesting & preserving: Purchase seeds or essential oil for household use. Use tender fresh leaves to flavor steamed fish as well as to warm in liquids. You can also use it as an ingredient in coffee cake batters.

Pests: aphids

Eucalyptus

Eucalyptus globulus

Smells are surer than sounds and
sights to make the heartstrings crack
—**Rudyard Kipling, "Lichtenberg," stanza 1**

Eucalyptus is native to the subtropical
dry forests of Australia and the leaves
of this plant are the favorite food of the
koala. The generic name *eucalyptus* is
derived from the ancient Greek words
eu, meaning "good" or "beautiful" and
kalypto, meaning "conceal" or "hide,"
referring to the caplike structure pro-
tecting emerging flower buds.

Eucalyptus, with its fragrant properties and evergreen foliage, makes
a wonderful addition to your indoor
environment, especially in the bedroom
and bath. Rated one of the top-ten
houseplants by NASA, eucalyptus is a
natural room freshener, filtering out
harmful compounds in the air, making it much healthier to breathe. Just
breathing in the aroma of this herb is
said to lower congestion and help ward
off colds.

Commercial production of eucalyptus oils began in 1860 in Victoria,
Australia, innovated by Joseph Bosisto,
an emigrant from England. Australia
Aboriginals used the bark and leaves in
various herbal remedies.

Eucalyptus globulus

Also called blue gum or Tasmanian
blue gum, this variety of eucalyptus is
famous for its antiseptic, germicidal,
and expectorant properties. Its large
oval leaves and stems have a silvery cast
and are very fragrant. Eucalyptus makes
a very ornamental, as well as useful,
houseplant.

Lemon eucalyptus
E. citriodora

The long, narrow green leaves of this
eucalyptus variety are hairy when young
and become smooth with age. It is a
very fast-growing plant. Its lemon scent
is quite strong and is an effective mosquito repellent.

Lemon eucalyptus

■ HERBAL LIFE

Simmer a handful of fresh eucalyptus leaves in 1 quart (960 ml) of water over low heat for 20 to 30 minutes to naturally disinfect and freshen indoor air quality during cold winter months.

■ LIVING WITH EUCALYPTUS

Common names: gum tree

Floral language: awakening, purifying

Description: fast-growing, large, evergreen tree featuring smooth drooping, dark-green, aromatic leaves

Growing conditions: Provide bright light, including direct sunlight, and keep soil evenly moist during summer's growing season. In winter, water when the top of the soil is dry. Despite its large height, the plant adapts well to an indoor environment if regularly pruned to keep its growth in check. Eucalyptus is a heavy feeder and will quickly outgrow its container and need to be repotted.

Propagation: not easily propagated; purchase plants as needed.

Plant parts used: leaves and leaf branches

Harvesting & preserving: Cut and hang branches in bundles and strip off leaves when dried. Use in potpourri, for crafts, and in flower arrangements.

Pests: susceptible to fungus gnats but, generally, relatively pest-free

Eucalyptus globulus

Lavender
Lavandula spp.

French lavender

> . . . let's go to that house; for the linen looks white, and smells of lavender, and I love to lie in a pair of sheets that smell so.
>
> —Izaak Walton, *The Compleat Angler*, 1653

The classic scent of lavender is almost universally recognized. This herb has been cherished, cultivated, and used from almost the beginning of recorded civilization. Native to the Mediterranean regions, the Middle East, and India, lavender is a fragrant silvery-green narrow-leaved perennial herb in the mint family. These decorative plants offer a wide variety of flower color, shape, and size

and some are more suitable to indoor culture than others.

Due to the plant's popularity and long history of use, lavender plants available for purchase today are mostly hybrids and cultivars.

Growing lavender indoors requires more care than other herbs. It must have plenty of light, excellent air circulation, and space. Lavender's genus name comes from the Latin word *lavare*, meaning "to wash," and since ancient times, lavender has been used for soaps and to perfume bath waters. A floral icon synonymous with tranquility, purity, and good housekeeping, lavender remains among the most versatile of all herbs. Aromatic, nostalgic, soothing, and healing, its flowers and foliage have a multiplicity of household uses. In aromatherapy, lavender essential oil is used in sedative and relaxing blends.

Lavender is notable for both its insect-repellent properties and long-lasting fragrance, and old herbalists were certain it cured everything from cramps to migraine, tremblings, and heart passions. In Tuscany, legend has it that lavender protects little children from the evil eye and the Kabyle women of North Africa believe it protects them from maltreatment by their husbands.

Success with growing lavender indoors begins with selecting a variety that will tolerate the growing conditions inside a home. The following are the most popular varieties for growing indoors as specimen plants and topiaries.

Spanish Lavender

Lavandula stoechas
Spanish lavender, also called French lavender or Italian lavender, has the most distinctive lavender flower. The flower heads resemble miniature pineapples and each one is tipped with a showy violet top knot of bracts resembling butterfly wings or rabbit ears. Greek botanist Dioscorides described this lavender in the first century AD as growing off Gaul's coast, now called Îles d'Hyères, a group of islands in the Mediterranean just off the southern coast of France. This is the lavender used medicinally and for toiletry purposes in the Middle Ages by the Romans. It is a tall upright lavender growing to 1½ feet (45 cm) indoors, with narrow gray-green leaves and a rosemary plant's overall appearance. Some of the best new cultivars appearing on the market come from this lavender species. They grow very well in containers indoors. This lavender has a pleasant camphor-rosemary scent and is ideal for making potpourri and sachets. Cooks occasionally use it in place of rosemary for seasoning grilled meats.

Spanish lavender

Lavandula × intermedia 'Grosso'

A lavandin cultivar 'Grosso' is a hybrid cross between English lavender and spike lavender and was discovered in the Vaucluse district of France in 1972. It is highly valued commercially because of its superior lavender aroma for soaps, room fresheners, candles, and culinary uses. It has one of the most delightful foliage colors of all the lavenders; its long tapered thick leaves are a lovely bold gray-green color with a bluish undertone. Unlike the other lavenders, this plant grows taller in height than in width and maintains a dense

'Goodwin Creek Gray'

well-behaved shape. The graceful flower stems curve gently outward from the plant with long deep dark-violet flower heads, a perfect accent to the compact rounded form of 'Grosso'. This plant is sometimes sold as "Fat Spike." It is a popular choice of lavender for topiaries, dried and fresh floral arrangements, DIY bath products, and culinary dishes.

Lavandula × *ginginsii* 'Goodwin Creek Gray'

This outstanding hybrid was discovered at Goodwin Creek Gardens by lavender specialist Jim Becker in 1999. This good-size plant's unique feature is its delightful silvery-green serrated leaves and it is valued ornamentally for its attractive soft-wooly foliage. The long spikes of deep purple flowers have a sweet fragrance but do not stand out as much as those of other lavenders. 'Goodwin Creek Gray' is often treated as a foliage plant; use as an accent plant, one properly placed plant will make a big impact. Easy to train as a standard. Plants grow 1 to 2 feet (30 to 60 cm) tall and wide.

■ HERBAL LIFE

True lavender (*Lavandula angustifolia*) is a lovely aromatic herb, prized for its diverse uses. Spike lavender (*L. latifolia*) is a pungent, camphor-scented herb and is cultivated primarily for its essential oil for use in cleaning products and insect repellents. Lavandin (*L.* × *intermedia*) is a hybrid of true lavender and spike lavender. Lavandin essential oil is less

LAVENDER AND ROSEMARY LAUNDRY RINSE

The mild acidic nature of vinegar makes it useful for a wide variety of cleaning tasks around the home. This simple laundry rinse will scent and rid your linens and clothes of excess soap residue.

1½ cups (weight varies, about 42 g) fresh lavender stems, leaves, and flowers

1½ cups (weight varies, about 48 g) fresh rosemary stems with leaves

8 cups (1.9 L) distilled white vinegar

1. In a gallon-size (3.8 L) glass jar, combine the lavender, rosemary, and vinegar. Seal the jar using a plastic lid or add a layer of wax paper or plastic wrap between the jar and a metal lid to avoid corrosion. Let the mixture steep in a warm, sunny window for 2 weeks.

2. Strain the herbs from the infusion and transfer the vinegar into a clean 2-quart-size (1.9 L) glass jar.

3. Add ½ cup (120 ml) infused vinegar to your final rinse cycle, or pour it into the fabric softener opening in your washer.

Yield: 2 quarts (1.9 L)

expensive than true lavender and is often used in place of true lavender in toiletries and household products.

■ LIVING WITH LAVENDER

Common names: lavandin, Lavandula, lavender

Floral language: constancy, devotion, distrust, luck, purity

Description: Lavenders are lovely, rounded, fragrant, silvery-leaved evergreen perennials. Depending on the variety, the flowers can be pink, pale to deep purple, or white. The foliage can range from blue green to almost gray. This bushy herb averages 1 to 2½ feet (30 to 75 cm) indoors and will live for 2 to 3 years.

Growing conditions: Grow lavender plants in fast-draining loose potting soil with a neutral pH and a light top-dressing of sand. A sunny south-facing window is essential; they must have 5 to 6 hours of direct sunlight daily. Additional artificial light is sometimes needed, even in the brightest of indoor settings. Be sure to water plants directly on the soil. Water on the foliage will lead to mold and pest infestations. Let the soil dry out between waterings. Prune plants after flowering even if you don't plan to harvest the flowers.

Propagation: Lavender is best propagated from cuttings.

Plant parts used: leaves and flowers

LAVENDER-OATMEAL SHOWER BAGS

Use these delightful-smelling bags to exfoliate skin while showering. You will need small muslin drawstring bags for this recipe.

1 cup (237 g) ground steel cut oats (colloidal oatmeal)

¼ cup (7 g) lavender buds

¼ cup (16 g) calendula flowers

2 tablespoons (2 8g) Himalayan salt

In a small bowl, stir together the oats, lavender, calendula flowers, and salt. Scoop the mixture into small muslin bags and tightly tie the bags closed.

Yield: 12 to 14 ounces (225 to 390 g)

Harvesting & preserving: To enjoy their aromatic properties, lavender's flowering stems should be harvested just as the flowers open. When snipping lavender stems, begin cutting at the bottom of the plant where the foliage begins. Hang the flower stalks or spread them on screens for a few days until dry. Use for scent in potpourris, floral arrangements, and aromatherapy. Lavender is used to flavor vinegar and culinary dishes by adventurous cooks.

Pests: fungus gnats

Tea Tree

Melaleuca alternifolia

How important is it to know the story of a plant? Some might say it's not important at all. However, I would suggest that if not for the reverence and first-hand knowledge of local gatherers over hundreds and thousands of years who selected specimens for superior flavor, healing capabilities, or striking beauty, that food, flower, or natural medicine would not be in your home today.

—**Justina Edwards, *The Planthunter***

Commonly known as Australian tea tree, *Melaleuca aternifolia*, is native to Australia's Bungawalbin Valley, in Northern New South Wales. The Indigenous Bundjalung People refer to the lands of the Bungawalbin as the "healing ground." The trees grow along the shores of freshwater lakes and the falling leaves and twigs stain the water a rich bronze hue and infuse it with tea tree's signature healing properties. The "protective" nature of these trees was so revered that tea tree lakes were reserved for women only and were sacred places used for child birthing.

The tree's aromatic leaves yield an essential oil with a fresh earthy scent valued for its antiseptic properties. It has been used in Australian traditional medicine for thousands of years.

Tea tree makes an attractive fragrant houseplant with a lot of personality and character. It can be trained as a standard or bonsai. This variety is the best known.

■ HERBAL LIFE

Numerous tea tree oil products are commercially available, including soap, toothpaste, shampoo, lip balm, and skin creams. Tea tree oil is one of the most popular essential oils used in aromatherapy.

■ LIVING WITH TEA TREE

Common names: the protector

Floral language: cleansing, purifying

Description: Tea tree is a small attractive evergreen tree with papery bark and delicate narrow soft needlelike leaves. The plant's indoor height is limited by the container size and regular pruning.

Growing conditions: Supply bright light, including direct sunlight. Always provide good drainage and never allow the soil to dry out completely. Reduce watering in winter. To counteract low humidity, place tea tree plants on top of a tray of gravel filled with water. Fertilize every month or so.

Propagation: Tea tree is best propagated by seed, or purchase nursery starts.

Plant parts used: leaves, fresh and dried

Harvesting & preserving: Mature leaves harvested from tea tree dry easily when spread in a single layer on a screen in a well-ventilated space out of direct sunlight. Store in an airtight glass container up to 1 year. Fresh or dried leaves may be infused in water or oil for medicinal and household uses.

Pests: mealy bugs

Catnip
Nepeta cataria

If you set it, the cats will eat it. If you sow it, the cats don't know it.
—**Ancient plant proverb**

Indigenous to Europe and Asia and extensively naturalized in North America, the genus name *Nepeta* is derived, depending on the sources, either from Nepi, a town in Italy, or nepa, a scorpion whose bite the plant supposedly could cure. Over the centuries, catnip has been attributed to amazing medicinal virtues—the power to combat giddiness, fever, and spasms—and its flowering tops were found to be "serviceable for nightmares." Numerous herbal preparations made with *Nepeta cataria* were put to use in Europe, the specific application varying with the plant part and the manner of concocting it. The oil expressed from the leaves was recommended to stimulate blood flow and the root, when chewed, was said to make the most gentle person fierce and quarrelsome.

In England, tea brewed from the leaves was the beverage of choice until teas from China supplanted it.

■ HERBAL LIFE

Catnip is universally recognized for its attractiveness to cats and the power of this herb is related to its distinctive pungent aroma. The pleasures of this ancient herb are not limited to felines. Catnip mixed with a bit of mint and lemon thyme is a very soothing tea for human coughs and colds.

■ LIVING WITH CATNIP

Common names: catnip

Floral language: "intoxication with love"

Description: A medium-size mint with aromatic heart-shaped gray-green serrated leaves and a bushy upright growth habit. The flowers of catnip are white with lavender spots and are found in clusters either at the stem tips or the leaf axils. Reaches 1 to 2 feet (30 to 60 cm) tall growing indoors.

Growing conditions: Supply bright light, including direct sunlight. Always provide good drainage but never allow the soil to dry out completely. Reduce watering in winter. Keep flowers pruned off to encourage lush foliage and prevent a sprawling growth habit. The cultivar 'Citriodora' resembles the species but has a refreshing lemon fragrance.

Propagation: by division, stem cutting, and seed

Plant parts used: leaves

Harvesting & preserving: Harvest small quantities of leaves anytime. Or cut plants back all the way to the base and tie the stems in bunches and hang them to dry in a well-ventilated room. When the leaves are crumbly dry, strip them off the stems and store in a glass jar. Catnip makes a soothing tea.

Pests: vulnerable to aphids, spider mites, whiteflies

Plectranthus

Plectranthus spp.

'Cerveza 'n Lime'

Plectranthus is a large South African genus in the mint family, sporting some 350 species of annuals, evergreen perennials, and semisucculent shrubs. A number of these plants are used for ornamental, food, and medicinal purposes. The genus name comes from the Greek words *plectron*, meaning spur, and *anthos*, meaning flower, in reference to the spur-shaped flowers of some species. A few make excellent houseplants.

Plectranthus coleoides 'Cerveza 'n Lime' is a hybrid closely resembling Cuban oregano, with its fuzzy, softly scalloped leaves and refreshing lime scent. Grown indoors, the plant reaches 14 to 18 inches (35 to 45 cm) high and 8 to 12 (20 to 30 cm) inches wide. It is a lovely easy-going indoor foliage plant.

Lemon leaf *Plectranthus* 'Mt. Carbine' is a new introduction from the Mt. Carbine area of Queensland, Northern Australia. The plant's sumptuous velvety leaves and luscious lemon scent are absolutely fabulous. You will not be able to resist stroking them and breathing in the fragrance. Try it in herbal syrups, iced tea, fruit salads, and spiced drinks. It is a very vigorous and easy-to-grow plant. Its upright growth habit reaches up to 2 feet (60 cm).

■ HERBAL LIFE

If you are having a bad day, lightly skim your fingers over Plectranthus's soft fuzzy foliage to set loose an uplifting mood-mending symphony of spicy citrus fragrance.

■ LIVING WITH PLECTRANTHUS

Common names: spur flower

Floral language: creativity

Description: There are many different types of Plectranthus, including species that are annuals, evergreens, shrubs, and perennials. All have attractive aromatic velvety foliage with scalloped or serrated edges and succulent stems. Plant height and width vary by species.

Growing conditions: Provide bright indirect sunlight and well-draining soil. Plectranthus are moderately tolerant of dry soil conditions. Water as needed and never let the plant sit in water. Pinch new stem tips regularly to keep the plant bushy.

Propagation: stem cuttings

Plant parts used: leaves, fresh or dried

'Mt. Carbine'

Harvesting & preserving: 'Cerveza 'n Lime' is valued for its fragrance and not for any culinary attributes. The fresh leaves of lemon leaf *Plectranthus* 'Mt. Carbine' can be used to garnish fruit dishes and to make a lemon-flavored herbal syrup.

Pests: seldom bothered by pests

Patchouli

Pogostemon cablin

Patchouli is a well-known essential oil with both physical and emotional properties and a fascinating history of use on many continents. —**Jeanne Rose,** **"Patchouli Essential Oil & Hydrosol"**

A tropical member of the mint family, patchouli is native to Indonesia, Malaysia, and India and has been cultivated for centuries for use as a perfume, aphrodisiac, and insect repellent. Its robust shrubby habit and attractive aromatic leaves make it an appealing addition to a fragrance garden, or an excellent houseplant. This square-stemmed, tender perennial produces small spikes of violet-tinged white flowers and deep-green oval serrated leaves. Drying patchouli leaves intensifies their herby fragrance. The name "patchouli" comes from the ancient Tamil word, *paccilai*, meaning "green leaf."

Although there are seventy-some species of patchouli, *Pogostemon cablin* is the plant best known as "true" patchouli. During the seventeenth and eighteenth centuries, elaborate hand-woven shawls from the East Indies came shipped to Europe packed in boxes layered with the leaves and stems of dried patchouli to protect the wares from insects. The fragrance of patchouli intensifies and mellows with age, so the shawls arrived at their destinations richly scented with the aroma of patchouli. The signature scent became synonymous with affluence and luxury, an aromatic seal of proof the shawls were authentic and from the East Indies. Napoleon's first wife, Josephine, was a big fan of patchouli perfume and this distinctive scent is often associated with the hippie era of 1960s and '70s.

Contemporary aromatherapists use patchouli oil to relieve stress and stress-related problems. It is important to note that although small quantities are uplifting and stimulating, larger doses of the plant's oil can have a sedative effect.

■ **HERBAL LIFE**

Dried patchouli leaves and orange peel blended make a simple but superbly scented potpourri. Breathing the plant's scent is said to cure apathy and indecision and help focus.

■ **LIVING WITH PATCHOULI**

Common names: kablin, pacha-pat or pot, true patchouli

Floral language: passion

Description: a bushy tender perennial averaging 18 inches (45 cm) tall and 12 inches (30 cm) wide

Growing conditions: Patchouli is a fast-growing plant that needs extra room to grow and frequent fertilization. It thrives in a warm, humid room that receives high to moderate light. This plant is very frost sensitive and prefers temperatures above 60°F (15.5°C), which makes it ideal for indoor growing. Keep the soil evenly moist but do not let it dry out between waterings.

Propagation: Patchouli is propagated by cuttings.

Plant parts used: leaves, fresh or dried

Harvesting & preserving: Prune the plant often to keep it bushy and compact. Mature patchouli leaves harvested from the plant are easily dried by spreading them in a single layer on a screen in a well-ventilated space out of direct sunlight. Use the leaves as a moth and insect repellent, in herbal sachets, and to make incense. Patchouli is a mood lifter; keep a fresh bouquet on your desk.

Pests: aphids, mealybugs, whiteflies

Houseleeks
Sempervivum tectorum

Houseleeks—thereby hangs a tale. Scores of our humblest plants, flowers, and herbs are the central characters in delightful legends and myths. One of the most common succulents, the sempervivum, along with the sedum, belong to the *Crassulaceae* family. "Semper," meaning *always living*, and "tectorum," meaning *of the roofs*. The succulent's thick leaves store water and can tough out droughts. This hardiness and resilience make the plant ideal for planting on rooftops where, once established, they do not need to be watered. Hens and chicks, as they are sometimes called, are planted on green roofs to help reduce air pollution, reduce storm water runoff, moderate temperature, and reduce urban noise.

One thing I could not figure out until recently is why my kid's books on herbs from Norway and Sweden contained between the pages on chamomile and hyssop, houseleeks. A little research cleared this up. —**Jane L. Taylor, children's garden designer,** "Houseleeks," *Michigan Herb Journal,* Spring 2004

According to legend, houseleeks were a gift to humans from the god Jupiter for protection from lightning, thunder, fire, and witchcraft. The Romans planted courtyards with pots of houseleeks and Charlemagne ordered them planted on the roofs to protect imperial goods and estates. They were also planted to help hold the roof slates in place. Houseleeks is also an ancient medicinal herb, with uses similar to aloe vera.

These are easy plants to grow indoors in containers or made into living wreaths.

■ **HERBAL LIFE**

Young girls in Sicily gathered the buds of houseleeks and named each bud for a possible lover. The fullest one that opened the next morning would identify her future husband.

■ **LIVING WITH HOUSELEEKS**

Common names: hens and chicks

Floral language: industry, vivacity

Description: Houseleeks, a succulent, produces a rosette of leaves with fibrous roots and a tendency to form clumps. The plant has fleshy, soft, green leaves, which may look glossy or matte. Smooth reddish runners extend small offsets outward.

Growing conditions: Provide bright light including direct sunlight and use a cactus potting mix. The plant is very tolerant of dry soil conditions. Water only as needed and never let the plant sit in water. Houseleeks produce small offsets, which develop roots and become separate plants.

Propagation: Separate the offsets or take leaf cuttings.

Plant parts used: Growing indoors this plant is valued for its decorative qualities, fun history of use, and fascinating folklore. *Not for flavor or fragrance.*

Harvesting & preserving: The word "leek" is from the Anglo-Saxon, *leac*, "a plant," so, "houseleek" literally means houseplant.

Pests: If properly cared for, succulents do not have many pests; occasionally fungus gnats and fungal crown rot are issues.

4.
Scented-Leaf Geraniums
(*Pelargonium* species)

And genteel geranium, with a leaf for all that come.

—Leigh Hunt

Scented-leaf *Pelargoniums* (geraniums), known for the extraordinary fragrance in their leaves, have been captivating gardeners for centuries. Native to Southern Africa, these tender perennials were first brought to Europe by English and Dutch botanists around 1632 and were introduced to colonial America before 1750. By 1870, they had become so popular that garden catalogs listed more than 150 varieties. These plants mimic the fragrances of flowers, foliage, fruits, and spices. The scent is contained in small beads of oil produced in glands in the base of tiny leaf hairs. The essential oil extracted from scented geranium leaves is used in the aromatherapy, perfume, and cosmetic industries. You can grow geraniums that smell like roses, nutmeg, peppermint, orange, lemon, and lime!

Cousins of the familiar bedding, or zonal, geraniums, scented geraniums have never been cultivated for their blossoms. Although pretty, they are not very large or brightly colored. Popularly known as scented-leaf, or fragrant-leaf, geraniums, these plants belong to the genus *Pelargonium*, whose name comes from the Greek word *pelargos*, for *stork*, descriptive of the geranium's long, narrow seed capsule. 'Storksbill' is also an old familiar name. *Pelargoniums* do belong to the geranium family, *Geraniaceae*, which also includes

cranesbills, such as 'Herb Robert' and other perennial geraniums.

Scented geraniums are easy to grow, both indoors and out. They come in a variety of shapes and sizes, each with a distinctive leaf form and texture. Their flowers, which vary in color, are shades of lavender, white, pink, salmon, and red and are generally small.

Scented geranium leaves are an essential ingredient in potpourri. They can be dropped into a punch for a scented garnish or used to flavor food. A few leaves of lemon or rose geranium placed in the bottom of a cake pan before pouring the batter in adds extra flavor to the cake. Drop a few leaves into the pot to brew along with your regular black or green tea. Scented geranium flowers are edible and excellent for candying and for garnishing desserts, beverages, and salads. Their fragrant leaves are lovely in fresh floral arrangements and hold up well. Try chopped leaves mixed into cake icing, too.

■ HERBAL LIFE
One of the first air fresheners, no self-respecting Victorian's windowsill would have been without a least one variety of scented geranium.

■ LIVING WITH SCENTED-LEAF GERANIUMS
Common names: pellies, storksbill

Floral language: hope, true friendship, unexpected meeting

Description: There are 100 or more scented geraniums varieties but only a few of these are true species. A few of the most familiar are apple, (*Pelargonium odoratissimum*), lemon (*P. crispum* and *P. citronellum*), rose, (*P. graveolens* and *P. capitatum*), and peppermint (*P. tomentosum*).

Growing conditions: Grow scented geraniums in a south-facing window that receives at least 4 hours of direct sunlight. Although plastic pots are convenient, scented geraniums grow best in clay pots. Keep them on the dry side; they like to dry out between waterings. Geraniums prefer a moderately rich, well-balanced potting soil amended with coarse sand or perlite to help with drainage. Some pelargonium species tend to get leggy, especially if not receiving enough sunlight. Keep plants pruned in pots tailored to the size of the plant. Feed with a balanced fertilizer, such as 15-15-15, during the growing season, tapering off during winter. Once a month, add 1 teaspoon magnesium sulfate to 1 gallon (3.8 L) fertilizer/water mix to provide magnesium if your fertilizer does not provide it.

Propagation: Cuttings are the best way to propagate scented geraniums. Take cuttings in January and February to increase your stock. Take cuttings in August for plants to overwinter inside, or to give as holiday gift plants. When taking cuttings, any buds or flowers should be removed from the cutting before rooting it.

Plant parts used: flowers and leaves

Harvesting & preserving: Leaves can be dried for crafts, potpourri, and fragrant sachets. Use fresh leaves to flavor sugar, herbal syrup, cakes, fruit salad, and teas.

Pests: Scented geraniums are resistant to most insects except whiteflies, which can be controlled with insecticidal soap.

ROSE-FRUIT CLAFOUTIS

If you do not have 'Rober's Lemon Rose', combine a few rose- and lemon-scented leaves. Serve this dish straight from the oven.

2 tablespoons (28 g) unsalted butter, melted

3 or 4 medium-size fresh *P*. 'Rober's Lemon Rose' leaves

¾ cup (150 g) sugar

¾ cup (93 g) all-purpose flour

¼ teaspoon salt

3 large eggs

1 cup (240 ml) milk

2 tablespoons (30 ml) orange- or lemon-flavored liqueur or extract

½ teaspoon pure vanilla extract

1 (14-ounce, or 395 g) can sliced peaches, drained

1 (14-ounce, or 395 g) pitted cherries, drained

1. Preheat the oven to 375°F (190°C, or gas mark 5). Evenly coat a 10-inch wide (25 cm), 2-inch (5 cm) deep pie plate with the melted butter. Set aside.

2. In a food processor or blender, blend the geranium leaves and sugar. Add the flour and salt. Mix until well blended.

3. In a small bowl, beat eggs and milk. Add the liqueur and vanilla and beat until combined.

4. With the food processor running, slowly pour the milk mixture into the flour and sugar mixture, blending, about 30 seconds. Pour the batter into the prepared pie pan.

5. Scatter the fruit over the top of the batter.

6. Bake for 45 to 50 minutes, or until the clafoutis is puffy and golden brown.

Yield: 6 to 8 servings

Recipe Courtesy Pat Crocker

'Rober's Lemon Rose'

◼ ROSE-SCENTED GERANIUMS

P. 'Rober's Lemon Rose'
Superlative sweet rose scent with overtones of citrus, *P*. 'Rober's Lemon Rose' is one of the loveliest of all the rose scents in the *graveolens* group. The plants have a bushy habit with tomato leaf–shaped leaves and sprays of pink flowers. Steep leaves in milk or sugar to add flavor to cakes and cookies. The leaves are useful both dried in potpourri and fresh in flower arrangements.

'Attar of Roses'

P. 'Attar of Roses'

The word *attar* comes from the Persian word for *strongly perfumed*, and 'Attar of Roses' aptly describes this cultivar's strong rose scent. It's a sizable plant, reaching 16 to 18 inches (40 to 45 cm) in height with a width of up to 30 inches (75 cm). Plant in a good-size pot, at least 2 to 4 inches (5 to 10 cm) in diameter, with room to grow. An enchanting rose-scented plant with slightly hairy, 3-inch (7.5 cm) lobed leaves and clusters of edible small lavender flowers. This geranium tends to branch out and needs to be pruned regularly.

FRAGRANT FLORAL WATER

Use this lovely floral water in place of rose-water in recipes to flavor cakes, cookies, and frostings. It also makes a refreshing facial mist and can be used in homemade body, bath, and hair care products. Rosemary, lavender, peppermint, thyme, and lemon balm also make lovely, fragrant floral water combinations.

1½ to 2 cups (144 to 192 g) chopped fresh rose-scented geranium leaves

2 cups (480 ml) filtered water

1. In a medium-size enamel or stain-less-steel saucepan over medium heat, combine the geranium leaves and water. Bring to a gentle boil. Cover the pan and adjust the heat to a simmer. Simmer for 30 minutes. Remove from the heat and let the infusion cool completely.

2. In a fine-mesh sieve set over a heatproof bowl, strain the geranium leaves from the water, pressing on the leaves to remove as much liquid from the leaves as possible. Transfer the floral water to a pint-size (480 ml) sterilized glass jar. Cover the jar and refrigerate for up to 1 to 2 weeks.

Yield: about 2 cups (480 ml)

OLD-FASHIONED ROSE GERANIUM AND PATCHOULI SALT SCRUB

A freshly scented exfoliant for keeping hands and feet soft and smooth.

1 cup (230 g) ground Himalayan salt

½ cup (48 g) finely chopped fresh rose geranium leaves

¼ cup (10 g) chopped fresh patchouli leaves

¾ cup (168 g) coconut oil

1. In a medium-size glass bowl, stir together all the ingredients until thoroughly mixed. Store in a quart-size (906 ml) Mason jar, or other glass container with a good seal, at room temperature and use within 2 to 3 months to maintain freshness.

Yield: 14 to 16 ounces (392 to 454 g)

'Rose'

P. 'Rose'

P. 'Rose' is the name given to many of the hybrid forms of P. 'Graveolens', commonly called 'Old-Fashioned Rose'. This is a sturdy plant with a branching upright growth habit and deeply cut green leaves and bright-pink flowers. The rose scent varies from plant to plant so be sure to brush the leaves and compare the scent of each plant before making your final selection. The rose-scented geranium, P. 'Reunion Rose' is a source of geraniol, which is used in perfumery as a less expensive substitute for rose oil, the fragrant essential oil distilled from rose petals.

'Gray Lady Plymouth'

P. 'Gray Lady Plymouth'

A vigorous-upright growing plant that easily reaches 24 to 30 inches (60 to 75 cm) tall, it is well suited for pot culture or the garden. The plant's colorful deeply divided gray-green leaves are variegated with white edging and splotches. The flowers are pink with striking purple stripes in the upper two petals. The fragrant rose-scented foliage lends color, fragrance, and interesting texture to fresh flower arrangements and herbal bouquets.

CRYSTALLIZED PELARGONIUM FLOWERS

The delicate flowers of scented geraniums make lovely garnishes on cakes, cookies, ice cream, and cheese plates. All scented geraniums have edible flowers.

Superfine sugar, for coating
Freshly picked scented geranium flowers
1 large egg white
Few drops water

1. Place the sugar in a saltshaker or in a fine-mesh sieve. Line a baking sheet or work surface with wax paper. Set aside.

2. Quickly rinse the flowers in cold water and place them on a paper towel to dry.

3. In a small bowl, whisk the egg white and water until smooth. Working one at a time, using tweezers to hold the flowers, gently dip them into the egg white. Some people prefer to use a paintbrush and paint the egg wash onto the flowers.

4. Shake the sugar over the coated flowers. Place the sugared flowers on the wax paper and let dry in a cool spot for several days. Store in an airtight container at room temperature for up to 1 year.

SCENTED GERANIUM SALAD DRESSING

This all-purpose dressing is great on Bibb lettuce and fruit salad. If you like things spicy, add the optional paprika for a little kick.

4 fresh lemon-scented geranium leaves

1 fresh apple-scented geranium leaf

1 fresh rose-scented geranium leaf

1 small fresh mint-scented geranium leaf

3 tablespoons (45 ml) white wine vinegar

1 tablespoon (12.5 g) sugar

1 teaspoon paprika (optional)

½ cup (120 ml) olive oil

1. In a blender, combine the geranium leaves, vinegar, sugar, and paprika (if using). Blend until completely smooth and incorporated.

2. With the blender running on low speed, in a slow, steady stream, pour in the olive oil, blending until emulsified. Refrigerate in an airtight container for 7 to 10 days. Shake before using.

Recipe Courtesy Kathleen Gipps
Yield: about 1 cup (240 ml)

Apple-scented

■ FRUIT-SCENTED GERANIUMS

Apple-Scented Geranium
P. odoratissimum

Odoratus is the Latin word for *fragrant*. It's the perfect description of this aromatic, award-winning geranium's fresh fruity apple scent. A true species, this compact spreading plant grows from a central rosette with a slightly tuberous root and reaches up to 12 inches (30 cm) high and 12 to 24 inches (30 to 60 cm) wide. The delightfully scented round, wavy-edged leaves are irresistible to touch. Trailing flower stems produce a profusion of tiny star-shaped, red-veined white flowers and the plant blooms almost continuously. It is a marvelous houseplant and is well suited to a hanging basket or pot. Provide bright light, including direct sunlight. The apple-scented geranium repels flies, especially if you brush the leaves occasionally to release their scent. I love this plant!

'Strawberry'

Strawberry-Scented Geranium 'Strawberry' *P.* 'Lady Scarborough' (Countess of Scarborough, Strawberry)

An easy-to-grow, semi-upright, densely branched variety of pelargonium, 'Strawberry' has small crinkled, sweetly scented leaves that smell like strawberries with a hint of citrus. This geranium's cheerful bright lavender-pink flowers are beautiful as well as edible. It reaches up to 2 feet (60 cm) tall; keep it pruned to maintain its bushy habit. Provide bright light, including direct sunlight. Also called 'Lady Scarborough', this charming hybrid was introduced in England before 1820. A lovely historical herbal houseplant, it is especially striking in hanging baskets if not heavily pruned. Dried leaves are superb in potpourri, or simply tucked between the pages of a letter to a friend.

POMEGRANATE-STRAWBERRY HERBAL SORBET

This refreshing sorbet is a snap to prepare and makes a splendid after-dinner dessert.

2 cups (480 ml) water
2 cups (400 g) sugar
8 fresh strawberry geranium leaves
6 fresh lemon verbena leaves
1 fresh 'Rober's Lemon Rose' leaf
2 cups (480 ml) pomegranate juice
¼ cup (60 ml) freshly squeezed lemon juice

1. In a 1-quart (960 ml) saucepan over high heat, bring the water to a boil. Stir in the sugar and geranium leaves. Reduce the heat to medium and simmer, stirring frequently, for 5 minutes, or until the mixture is reduced to a light syrup. Remove from the heat and set aside to cool.

2. In a large bowl, stir together the cooled simple syrup, pomegranate juice, and lemon juice. Cover and refrigerate until cold.

3. Transfer to an airtight container and freeze until firm, about 2 hours. Keep frozen in an airtight, freezer-safe container for up to 6 months.

Yield: 4 to 6 servings

Lemon-scented

P. crispum

■ CITRUS-SCENTED GERANIUMS

Lemon-Scented Geranium
***P. citronellum* (formerly known as
P. 'Mabel Gray')**

P. citronellum is a large bushy plant
with palm-shaped, deeply lobed,
coarsely textured green leaves and a
marvelous lemon fragrance. It produces
small, pretty pink flowers stippled with
deep-purple markings on the two upper
petals. Its upright growth can reach
nearly 4 feet (120 cm). Keep plants
pruned to encourage branching and
control height. This is a perfect variety
to train to a single-stem topiary. A sunny
windowsill is best; avoid low light and
north-facing windows. Place the plant
where you will brush against it and
release its lovely scent. Tasty for tea, dec-
orating desserts, and adding to sorbets.
Lemon geranium leaves are beautifully
dried or pressed for herbal projects and
potpourris.

Lemon-Scented Geranium
P. crispum

This fabulous pelargonium has a neat,
upright semitrailing growth habit reaching to 2 feet (60 cm) tall, with small,
crinkly, three-lobed green leaves with
an intense lemon scent. Its bi-colored
pink blooms are surprisingly large and
very showy. Named 'The Finger Bowl' by
Victorians, this geranium is the traditional variety used in finger bowls placed
beside each dinner plate for guests to dip
their fingers into between courses. This
lovely old-fashioned scented geranium
has long been favored for topiary standards. Use fresh leaves to flavor desserts,
fruit dishes, and herb vinegar and dried
leaves in potpourris and for herb pillows.

LEMON GERANIUM MOUSSE

This light and refreshing mousse is good any time but particularly on a hot summer evening. The cream is heated only to infuse the flavor of the lemon peel and lemon-scented geranium leaves.

⅔ cup (180 ml) heavy cream

Finely grated zest of 1 lemon

6 fresh lemon-scented geranium leaves, plus more for garnish

¾ cup (150 g) superfine sugar

4 large eggs, separated

Juice of 1 lemon

⅔ cup (160 ml) water

1 (0.25-ounce, or 7 g) envelope unflavored gelatin

Fresh lemon-scented geranium flowers, for garnish

1. In a medium-size sauce pan over medium-low heat, gently heat the heavy cream, lemon zest, and geranium leaves just until the cream begins to steam. **Do not boil.** Remove from the heat and let cool.

2. In a medium-size bowl, using a handheld mixer, beat the sugar and egg yolks until thick. Add the lemon juice and beat to combine.

3. Place the water in a small saucepan and sprinkle the gelatin on the water. Place the saucepan over low heat and cook, stirring, until the gelatin has dissolved completely, 5 to 10 minutes.

4. While whisking constantly and pouring from 2 feet (60 cm) above the egg yolk mixture, fold the gelatin into the egg yolks, then set aside until the mixture begins to thicken, about 30 minutes (it thickens as it cools).

5. Using a fine-mesh sieve set over a medium-size bowl, strain the cooled cream to remove the zest and leaves. Using a handheld mixer, whip the cream until slightly thickened, then fold it into the mousse mixture.

6. In a large bowl and using a handheld mixer, beat the egg whites until stiff peaks form. Fold the beaten whites into the mousse.

7. Pour the mousse into individual dessert dishes or ramekins and chill thoroughly until set.

8. Garnish with fresh geranium leaves and flowers before serving.

Recipe Courtesy Donna Frawley
Yield: 6 to 8 servings

'Orange'   'Lime'   'Chocolate peppermint'

Orange-Scented Geranium
P. 'Orange'

P. 'Orange' is a medium-size variety with an upright, compact growth habit and bright-green serrated fan-shaped leaves and a delightful orange fragrance. Its large, showy flowers are light pink with deep-purple streaks on the upper petals. This plant is easily grown indoors with plenty of bright light. An upright grower reaching up to 2 feet (60 cm) tall, P. 'Orange' welcomes frequent grooming. The citrusy orange-scented leaves may be infused to make tea and used fresh to flavor desserts, fruit dishes, and herb vinegar; use dried leaves in potpourris and for herb pillows.

Lime-Scented Geranium
P. 'Lime'

A pelargonium hybrid of ancient origins, P. 'Lime' is an excellent container plant and a very accommodating houseplant in a sunny window. Strong, upright stems hold small, slightly rounded, smooth dark-green ruffled leaves with a delightful lime scent. The flowers are larger than most pelargoniums and are pale lavender with dark-purple spots on the upper petals. The plant's sturdy growth habit makes it an ideal candidate for training as a fragrant tabletop topiary. This plant will grow tall and lanky if not pruned frequently. A slight brush of its citrus-scented leaves will instantly lift your spirits. Take care not to over-prune this fragrant plant. Leaves may be infused to make tea and used fresh to flavor desserts, fruit dishes, and herb vinegar; use dried leaves in potpourris and for herb pillows.

■ MINT-SCENTED PELARGONIUMS

Peppermint-Scented Geranium
P. tomentosum

This remarkable species of pelargonium has been cultivated for hundreds

PEPPERMINT CHERRY TEA SANDWICHES

8 ounces (225 g) cream cheese, at room temperature

¾ cup (120 g) chopped dried cherries

¼ cup (23 g) chopped almonds

1 tablespoon (4 g) chopped fresh peppermint pelargonium (*P. tomentosum*) leaves

In a small bowl, thoroughly mix all the ingredients until combined. Spread on your favorite bread. Refrigerate leftovers in an airtight container for 2 to 3 days.

of years. Named for its huge velvety dark-green leaves, *tomentosum* is Latin for *thickly haired*. Famous English garden writer Gertrude Jekyll describes *P. tomentosum* leaves as "thick as a fairy blanket, and soft as a vicuna robe." Children find the plant's strong mint scent and large leaves irresistible. This peppermint pelargonium is a perfect plant to spark a child's interest in growing things. A vigorous grower, this plant has a sprawling and trailing growth habit and small white flowers. Peppermint geranium likes 5 to 6 hours of bright light a day, including direct sunlight, and a large, well-drained container with evenly moist soil conditions. Use the fresh leaves in teas, punches, and as a flavoring ingredient for pound cakes and chocolate puddings. The dark green leaves' undersides are gray, making an attractive complement of colors in a fresh flower arrangement. Dried leaves are great in potpourri.

Chocolate Mint–Scented Geranium

P. 'Chocolate Peppermint'

The term "chocolate" often refers more to the color of a plant than the plant's scent, as in the case of chocolate mint-scented geranium. Its soft, fragrant, velvety leaves are a vibrant herby green with dark-colored central splotches, referenced as chocolate in this plant's name. It produces small insignificant lavender-pink flowers. Because of its sprawling growth habit and exuberant personality, give this plant room to grow; it reaches 20 inches (50 cm) tall and 24 inches (60 cm) wide. Let the soil mix dry completely before watering, then give it a good soaking and allow the water to drain. Provide 4 to 5 hours of bright light, including direct sunlight, daily. I value this plant for its ornamental and fragrant qualities and do not use it for cooking.

5.
Temporary House Guests and Herbal Topiaries

One plant in a tin can may be a more helpful and inspiring garden to some people than a whole garden of flowers may be to another. It depends on the temperament of the person.
—**L.H. Bailey,** *Garden-Making*

Even with the most diligent care, plants growing indoors eventually decline and need to be replaced. As Charles A. Lewis, in his classic book *Green Nature/Human Nature: The Meaning of Plants in Our Lives*, perceptively states, "Plants and people share the rhythm of life. They both evolve and change, respond to nurture and climate, and live and die." Some plants manage to adapt readily to an indoor environment and thrive for years with little effort on your part. But not all houseplants are long-lived, especially certain herbs. The important thing is to enjoy them while you have them and replace them as needed.

Generally speaking, there are a few basic types of indoor herbal houseplants people like to use throughout their homes.

1. Transients
Transients are indoor plants we use the same way as annuals in the garden for short-season displays. Often gift plants associated with seasonal celebrations, they bring temporary pleasure and are here and gone.

2. Hardy long-lived decorative plants
We buy these plants purely for decorative reasons, to improve the appearance of a particular space or room in the home. Because you know exactly where the plant will live, you select plants suited to the particular indoor environment and lighting. Cardamom, scented geraniums, and many perennial herbs covered previously in this book (see chapters 3 and 4) are easy-going long-lived plants indoors, if given the proper environment, soil, nutrients, and lighting.

3. Plants valued as good friends
We enjoy spending the time and effort to create the perfect environment suited to each of these plant's individual needs because we think of them as friends.

Lemon verbena (*Aloysia citriodora*), a lovely tender perennial herb, emits an extraordinary lemon fragrance when you brush the leaves. Native to Argentina and Chile, it is a deciduous shrubby herb with woody stems. It grows 2 to 3 feet (60 to 90 cm) tall in my garden, but in its natural habitat, it reaches 10 to 15 feet (300 to 450 cm) tall. The fresh or dried leaves make a soothing, delicious tea and are also used to flavor liqueurs, custards, sauces, stuffings, and salads. Before the last frost of the season, I harvest the leaves to dry for potpourri and winter aromatherapy, their strong lemon scent lasts 2 to 3 years.

Lemon verbena is not only tender, it's also temperamental. Because it is a deciduous plant, it resents seasonal change and promptly drops its leaves when brought inside for the winter. What's more, it's a whiny, leggy, and demanding plant indoors. This quirky behavior does not bother my friend Carole; she loves this plant and enjoys the challenge of growing it as a houseplant. She tends her lemon verbena plant in a bright sunless window, eagerly awaiting the new leaves to emerge in late winter. Many herb gardeners like myself think it is easier to purchase a new plant each spring. It all depends on your temperament, and because there are always exceptions, you may well be the one person

Lemon verbena

out of 100 who can grow a specific herb indoors. Do not be afraid to experiment.

I have my select group of good friend plants I host regularly. For instance, I love Corsican mint, *Mentha requienii*, a creeping herbaceous perennial with tiny, dark-green, heart-shaped leaves strongly scented of pennyroyal and peppermint. Native to the islands of Corsica, France, and Sardinia, Italy, people often mistake Corsican mint for the houseplant called baby tears or some type of moss. In Mother Nature's world—one size does not fit all—it's a miniature mat-forming mint and, indoors, hardly reaches 1 inch (2.5 cm) in height. Like all mints, it does well with low indirect sunlight. I never grow tired of this plant; if you lightly stroke the leaves, they release an uplifting, enchanting minty aroma. It makes a lovely ground cover in a small dish or fairy garden. Because it is a short-lived plant, I replace my Corsican mint annually, or as needed.

Corsican mint

Indoor Herbal Gardens

Indoor gardens are groups of plants planted together, rather than showcased as individual specimens. They are containers filled with several plants, designed to highlight the color, texture, scent, and growth habit of each herb. "Gardens do not have to be measured in feet, yards or acres, they can be measured in inches just as successfully," says Mary Mason Campbell in her delightful book, *Kitchen Gardens*— and people have been doing just that for thousands of years. One of the Seven Wonders of the Ancient World was the Hanging Gardens of Babylon. According to legend, the queen of Babylon was homesick for the lush verdant land where she was born and raised and so implored her husband, King Nebuchadnezzar, to ease her pain and build a garden. So, to console his wife, he built the Hanging Gardens.

When creating an indoor herbal garden, it's important to choose plants with similar cultural needs because all the plants receive the same amount of moisture and light. Creatively approached, growing a group of herbs together in a single pot offers a great opportunity to experiment with theme gardening, grow plants that extend your personal interests, or indulge whims and fancies.

Keep in mind, the plants will eventually outgrow the space. Your container's diameter should be about 2 inches (5 cm) larger than the total diameter of all the pots you're combining. As the garden ages, prune or remove plants to avoid overcrowding. Close planting reduces air circulation and the chance of a pest or disease attack increases. Keep plants groomed and pruned to fit the available space.

A collection of lemon-scented herbs

Herbal Topiary

The art and craft of topiary can be traced back to imperial Rome. It is believed that topiary was invented by Gaius Matius, a Roman knight and a friend to Julius Caesar. Following the decline of the Roman Empire, the art of topiary fell out of favor until medieval times, as cities were enclosed behind castle walls, people needed to combine space savings with beauty, and kept trees and shrubs creatively pruned and shaped. From there, Europeans continued to practice and develop their topiary skills, branching out to create hunting scenes, mazes,

and whimsical follies. In the late 1600s, topiary was introduced in America.

Decorative botanical accents, herb topiaries are among the most versatile types of indoor garden plants, as they can be moved about your home easily. Standing alone or grouped together, they are guaranteed to dress up a table or room for any festive occasion. Bearing in mind when the party is over, everyone goes home, including the topiaries, returning to their sunny window. Herbal topiaries are long-lived if provided a growing location with reliable strong light and cool temperatures. Never allow

Myrtle

the soil mix to dry completely before watering.

Ready-made topiaries are available for purchase year-round, or you can grow your own. There are three categories of tabletop topiary: standards, hollow, and stuffed topiaries. I like standards because of their pleasing simplicity and resemblance to small lollipop-shaped trees. Single-stem standards are most often seen in pairs and seem to enjoy companionship. They look especially at home on either side of a fireplace or arranged on a table in staggering heights like a group of candlesticks.

TWO PLANTS FOR HERBAL TOPIARIES

Two are better than one because they have good return for their labor.
—**Ecclesiastes 4:9, NAS Bible**

Myrtle (*Myrtus communis*)

An ancient herb native to the Mediterranean and southwest Europe, myrtle is one of the top plants used for topiary, especially for training as a standard or other unique single-stem topiary shape. A handsome subtropical shrub with tiny narrow shiny bright-green leaves, the foliage releases a spicy smell when cut or brushed. The plant's charming aromatic white flowers sport pretty gold stamens. After blooming, they are followed by delicate blue-black berries. Myrtle is so sweetly scented that, according to ancient legend, when Adam was expelled from paradise, he was allowed to take with him wheat, the primary of foods; date, the ultimate of fruits; and myrtle, the chief of scented flowers. The Greeks and Romans substituted myrtle for bay as a seasoning. Myrtle was also used with bay or in place of bay for wreaths presented to poets and other highly regarded citizens, symbolizing love and immortality. In the Bible, it often signifies peace and love. Grecian myrtle is one of the common names of *M. communis* and its long history of use is deeply intertwined with mythology. Myrtle groves are a traditional scene in Italian paintings as a backdrop for the figure of Venus, the goddess of love. Legend has it that when satyrs were pursuing Venus and her nymphs, they found refuge in a grove of myrtle trees. Today, it is often used in wedding bouquets and wedding flowers, signifying "be my love" in floral language.

Myrtle is a great houseplant if provided bright, indirect sunlight and slightly evenly moist soil conditions. It's important to keep your standards pruned; regular snipping and clipping will maintain a standard shapely and lush. Keep the inside of the head cleared out to increase air circulation. Cut out dead twigs and thin live growth so light and air can penetrate the middle of the topiary. Plants should be repotted when their roots outgrow their present containers. If you must water plants daily, this is a good indication the plant needs to be repotted into a larger pot.

Gray Santolina

Gray Santolina (Santolina chamaecyparissus)

Also called lavender cotton (though in no way related to the cotton plant or lavender), Gray Santolina is a medieval ornamental herb once valued as a fumigant against moths. It was also reputed to resist poison, decay, and heal the bites of venomous beasts, according to Nicholas Culpeper's *Complete Herbal*, published in 1653.

Gray Santolina's finely serrated leaves are densely packed on stiff stems and resemble delicate bundles of gray coral. If properly trained, it will grow upright, resembling a little decorative tree that reaches a foot or so (about 30 cm) in height. Lavender cotton must have good air circulation, so it's important to avoid crowding it with other plants. It needs at least 5 to 6 hours of direct sunlight daily. Water when dry. Good drainage is essential—be careful not to overwater. Keep the foliage pruned and promptly remove brown and dead leaves. Save and dry the leaves of Santolina and mix them with dried mint and lavender to create a fragrant herbal blend. Stuff into small muslin bags to repel moths and scent closets and drawers. Its gray-coral branches are attractive in fresh flower arrangements and "talking" bouquets (see page 164). In the language of flowers, Santolina signifies protection and wards off evil. When growing indoors, Santolina is a short-lived plant.

RAISING STANDARD TOPIARIES FROM ROOTED STEM CUTTINGS

It takes time and patience to start new topiaries and due diligence to train them to do what doesn't come naturally to a plant, but it's a fun project that satisfies your creative appetite.

1 straight-stemmed herb cutting

Small clay pot

Soil-based potting mix

Wooden or bamboo stake

String, raffia, or twine

Pruning shears

1. The best herb cuttings to use for topiaries are shrubby ones, as woody stems give your standard strength. Rosemary, myrtle, bay laurel, Santolina, scented-leaf geraniums, and lavender are great perennial herbs for training as topiary. Choose a rooted cutting with a naturally upright habit to make it easier to get a straight erect stem. Use unpinched leafy cuttings without flower buds or part of the flower stalk.

2. Fill a small pot with a well-draining soil-based mixture and water it thoroughly.

3. Place the herb cutting into the potting mixture and firmly anchor it with a wooden or bamboo stake inserted alongside the erect stem. Starting from the bottom of the cutting, gently tie the stem to the stake at intervals where it needs straightening and support.

4. Pinch off the terminal, or end, bud from the main stem once the plant reaches the desired height. It's time to control the upward growth and begin to develop the topiary's form. Snip off the tips of the side shoots growing on the top one-third of the plant stems once the shoots reach 1 to 2 inches (2.5 to 5 cm) in length. Make the cut just above the set of leaves below the leaf tip.

5. Continue removing any stems that start to grow on the lower two-thirds of the plant. The plant should be moved to a larger pot when the roots outgrow the present container.

6. Follow with a thorough watering, then let the soil dry out before watering again. Wait to fertilize the topiary until it has acclimated to its new pot and is putting out lots of new growth. It's important to keep young topiaries pruned as they grow to ensure a pleasing shape. Frequent pruning encourages dormant bud growth, which is an essential element to a strong well-balanced topiary.

MAKING A FAUX HERBAL TOPIARY

You can also use fresh flowers and foliage or artificial plant materials to create faux topiary-inspired floral arrangements. Don Haynie, herb expert and floral designer extraordinaire, developed the idea for this whimsical faux herbal topiary when he was working in the floral industry in Virginia, United States. He was doing flowers for a wedding and the bride wanted to use the same wedding reception floral arrangements the night before, then give them as gifts to her wedding party. A tall order for a florist to fill because Don was concerned the arrangements would not last several days, let alone being toted about to several locations. Then, one night, his guardian angel appeared to him in a dream flying around the room on a bathroom plunger, and he got up and jotted the idea down. Don has graciously shared the original directions on how to make this faux topiary. Any seasonal combination of fresh flowers, herbs, and foliage may be used.

1 brick floral foam, divided

Suitable container for a base, such as a clay or terra-cotta pot

Fine gravel

Bathroom plunger, large or small

Generous handful sheet moss (1 bag is ample)

5 or 6 greenery pins

Generous handful Spanish moss (1 bag is ample)

2 medium-size rubber bands

Vine (such as ivy or grape vine), enough to wind around the plunger handle

15 to 20 herb cuttings (such as rosemary, lavender, and scented geraniums), 2 to 8 inches (5 to 20 cm) long

12 to 15 flowers of choice

1. Tightly wedge a piece of floral foam brick into the container and pack gravel around it to add stability.

2. Insert the plunger handle into the center of the foam, pushing it down firmly. If the handle is too tall to be in scale with the container, cut off a section.

3. Dampen the sheet moss and use it to cover the foam in the container, securing it with the greenery pins.

4. Cut the remaining floral foam to fit and fill the plunger cup.

5. Dampen the Spanish moss and let it sit for about 30 minutes, or until pliable. Cover the plunger cup and the foam inside completely with clumps of the dampened Spanish moss. Secure the moss with rubber bands placed on opposite sides of the plunger cup and stretched up and over the top.

6. Moisten the floral foam in the container, which is now covered with moss.

7. Insert the lower end of the vine into the foam in the container and loosely wind the vine up the plunger handle. Secure the end of the vine beneath the plunger bowl with string or wire if it slips.

8. Moisten the foam in the plunger cup and begin arranging flowers and herbs in it.

9. Start with base material, such as rosemary or scented geraniums, and let some droop over the edge. Fill it in but don't pack it—keep it loose. Then intersperse the base flowers and herbs with more flowers (roses or daisies work well) throughout.

10. Don't push the stems too far into the foam; you want the flowers to show through the herbs. Finish the arrangement with baby's breath, statice, or other wispy herbs.

Yield: 1 topiary, or as many as needed

6 .
Preserving Your
Herbal Harvest

PART 1
GUIDELINES FOR HARVESTING AND
PRESERVING INDOOR HERBS

To grow them is to know them, to know them is to use them, to use them is to love them, then happily herbs become your way of life.
—**Bertha Reppert,** *Growing and Using Herbs with Confidence*

The real beauty of herbs emerges when you get up close and personal with the plants. Knowing when and how to harvest them involves an intimate connection and firsthand knowledge of each plant's natural life cycle and reproductive habits. We can all benefit from a daily dose of green enchantment. Ultimately herbs appeal to each of the five senses and have something of value to satisfy the mind, body, and spirit of every person. Harvesting can begin anytime there is sufficient foliage on the plant to tolerate cutting. Except for annual herbs at the end of their growing season, never cut back a plant completely when harvesting it.

Rules for Herbal Harvesting

Follow these tips for the most bountiful harvest.

- Indoors, most herbs put out new growth at the tips of their branches and this is where they should be pinched to encourage a bushier shape. Use herbs fresh, or dry for later use. Some herbs, such as chives, parsley, or sorrel, grow from the base of the plant, so snip the older leaves growing outside first. Be careful not to overharvest the plant, especially during the slow winter season.

- If your herbal houseplants are summering outdoors, harvest them in the morning after any dew has dried and before the sun gets too hot. To harvest properly, cut stems. Do not pull leaves from the plant.

- Pick healthy growth and discard damaged flowers and leaves.

- Only harvest what you have time to prepare and use.

- Wash, dry, and preserve herbs as quickly as possible after harvesting them.

- When harvesting herbs grown for their flavorful leaves, harvest the leaves just before the plant flowers.

- Harvest flowers for drying before they're fully opened.

- Harvest seeds when they're fully ripened. For this, you can cut the whole plant or just the seed stalk/head.

Preserving and Using Herbs

There are several methods you can use to preserve and enjoy your herbal harvest. Here are some of my favorites.

TECHNIQUES FOR AIR-DRYING HERBS

- Tie large leafy-stemmed herbs with rubber bands into loose bundles and hang them in a room or closet with good cross air circulation. Herb bundles tend to shrink and loosen as they dry—check them and tighten each bundle as needed. Depending on the herb, drying time ranges from 2 days to several weeks for the herbs to completely dry. They should feel crisp when fully dry.

- Strip the fresh leaves or flowers from the plant stems and spread them in a thin layer on screens. You can use a house window screen lined with cheesecloth or paper towels. Place screens in a well-ventilated area and let the herbs dry. Stir the herbs and spread them out again several times a day to speed drying times.

- Hang plants harvested for seeds upside-down to dry with the flower/seed heads enclosed in paper bags to catch dropping seeds.

- Store completely dried herbs in clean glass jars away from heat and light to preserve their flavors and fragrances. Be sure to check for moisture before putting freshly dried herbs into jars.

There are three main ways to preserve
herbs by freezing them.

- Carefully chop fresh-cut herbs with
  a kitchen knife or kitchen shears.
  Evenly spread the herbs on a baking
  sheet lined with parchment paper
  and place it in the freezer for several
  hours. Pack the frozen herbs in
  small containers, label and date the
  containers, and keep frozen for 6 to 8
  months.

- Freezing herbs in stock or water
  works well for preserving herbs for
  use in stews and dishes with high
  water content. Place finely chopped
  fresh herbs in water or broth in the
  desired concentration and freeze in
  ice-cube trays. Remove the frozen
  cubes from trays and place in zip-top
  bags. Keep frozen until needed.

  You can freeze whole edible flowers
  by placing them in ice-cube trays.
  Fill an ice-cube tray half full of water,
  then place the edible flowers face-
  down in the water and finish filling
  the tray with water. Freeze until firm.
  Transfer to zip-top bags. Keep frozen
  until needed.

- To freeze herbs in oil, blend 2 cups
  (weight varies) finely chopped fresh
  herbs into ½ cup (120 ml) good-
  quality oil. The oil acts as a carrier for
  the herbs, so use just enough oil to
  bind the mixture. Pack the herb oil
  into small airtight containers, label
  and date your containers, and freeze
  for up to 1 year. Chip or scrape off
  what is needed for each dish. Herbs
  in oil must be kept frozen until use.

PART 2
HERB RECIPES FOR USE AND DELIGHT

It is the plants themselves that linger over the centuries, entwining various periods of garden history with a repetitive theme. Old sources are resuscitated in so many guises.
—Kay N. Sanecki, *The History of the English Herb Garden*

As you're about to learn, there are many ways to use herbs in the kitchen and around your home. This part of the book is dedicated to ways you can enjoy your herbal houseplant harvest, including recipes for cooking, crafting, and beauty care.

Herbs for Flavor

Breads, Cakes, Pastries: All savory seeds, dill weed, marjoram, parsley, sage, savory, shallots

Cheese, Hot Dishes: Basil, cumin, marjoram, oregano, sage, tarragon, thyme

Cream or Cottage Cheese: Basil, caraway, chives, dill weed, mint, parsley sage, savory

Tomato Cocktail: Basil, dill weed, marjoram, savory, tarragon, thyme

Egg Dishes: Basil, chervil, chives, marjoram, savory, tarragon, thyme

Desserts: Anise, caraway, coriander, marjoram, mint, poppy seed, sesame

Fish: Basil, bay leaf, chervil, chives, fennel, lemon thyme, parsley, tarragon, thyme

Fruit Cup and Cold Beverages: Borage, burnet, lemon balm, lemon thyme, lemon verbena, mint, rose geranium, rosemary

Meats

Beef: Garlic, marjoram, savory, shallots, thyme, rosemary

Lamb: Dill weed, fennel, garlic, marjoram, mint, rosemary, savory

Pork: Basil, chives, marjoram, rosemary, sage, shallots

Poultry: Marjoram, parsley, rosemary, sage, savory, tarragon

Salad Dressing: All savory seeds, basil, chervil, dill weed, garlic, parsley, shallot, tarragon

Salads: Caraway, chervil, chives, dill weed, lemon balm, lovage, mint, parsley, salad burnet, savory, shallot, thyme

Soups: Celery, chervil, lovage, marjoram, parsley, savory, thyme

Stews: Bay leaf, lovage, marjoram, parsley, rosemary, shallot, thyme

Veal: Rosemary, sage, savory, thyme

Vegetables

Beets: Basil, caraway, fennel, mint, savory, tarragon

Cabbage: Caraway, dill weed, fennel, mint, thyme

Carrots: Basil, dill weed, fennel, mint, parsley, savory, thyme

Onions: Marjoram, sage, tarragon, thyme

Peas: Basil, mint, rosemary, summer savory

Potatoes: Basil, celery seed, chives, dill weed, lovage, mint, parsley

Spinach: Garlic, marjoram, mint, rosemary

String Beans: Marjoram, sage, savory

Summer Squash: Basil, marjoram, oregano, thyme

Thyme and marjoram are a good combination for many vegetables. Parsley and chives are great together.

Tomato: Basil, bay leaf, fennel, marjoram, oregano, sage, tarragon, thyme

THYMELY TIPS AND SAGE ADVICE FOR USING HERBS

- Herbs are meant to enhance the flavor of food, not smother or overpower it. Do not add herbs to taste, but merely for a touch of flavor. The general rule is ½ teaspoon dried herbs in a recipe per 4 servings. Use 4 times as much of a fresh green herb. The right amount of herb for your family may vary from this rule. Too little is better than too much; start with a "pinch" and add more after letting the herb's flavor mingle and mix with the other ingredients.

- Fresh herbs are heavenly. Any herb can be used fresh for seasoning food, mixing with salad greens, or brewing tea. Soft green stems can be used but woody stems should be discarded. Freshly cut herbs will last 3 to 4 days when wrapped in a damp towel placed in a plastic bag and kept refrigerated.

- The longer an herb is in a dish, the more of the herb's volatile oil that is released, so allow time for flavor to develop. Heat brings out flavor more quickly than cold, so add herbs to cold dishes, vegetables, cocktails, butters, or cheese spreads several hours to overnight before serving. Don't worry about the "proper" herb. Blessed are the curious for they shall have an adventure.

Quick and Simple Ways to Use Herbs

MAKING A BASIC HERB BUTTER

Herb butter may include any single herb or a combination of several.

Combine 2 or 3 tablespoons (weight varies) finely chopped fresh herbs with 1 cup (2 sticks, or 224 g) unsalted butter, at room temperature. Some cooks like to add 1 tablespoon (15 ml) olive oil to give the herb butter a more spreadable texture. You can also add a pinch of salt or a squeeze of fresh lemon juice. Pack the butter into a small crock or roll it into a log, using plastic wrap as an aid, for slicing. Refrigerate the herb butter in an airtight container for about 3 weeks, or freeze for up to 3 months.

HERB-INFUSED VINEGAR

Clean, unblemished fresh herb leaves, seeds, roots, and flowers can all be used to flavor vinegars, depending on the recipe. Make sure your herbs are thoroughly washed and dried before placing them into the vinegar. Use a high-quality vinegar within an acidity level no lower than 5 percent.

Combine the ingredients in a ratio of ½ to 1 cup (weight varies) herbs to 2 cups (480 ml) vinegar.

Place the herb parts in a clear glass container, pour the vinegar over them, and tightly close the container. Let sit for several weeks for the flavor of the herb parts to infuse the vinegar.

Strain the herbs from the vinegar and rebottle the vinegar. Use a plastic lid or add a layer of wax paper or plastic wrap to the bottle top before placing the cap on the bottle to avoid a metal lid corrosion.

SIMPLE HERBAL SYRUP

Basil, bay, lemon balm, mint, rosemary, and scented geraniums all make tasty ingredients for herbal syrups. The amounts of herbs used in simple syrups will vary depending on the flavor of each herb and personal preference. Use herbal syrups for sweetening teas, drinks, cocktails, and punches or as an ingredient in dressings for fruit salads.

> 2 cups (400 g) sugar
> 2 cups (480 ml) water
> 1 cup (weight varies) herb sprigs

In a medium pan, combine all the ingredients and bring to a soft boil. Simmer for 5 minutes, stirring occasionally, until the sugar dissolves. Remove from the heat and let cool thoroughly. Strain the herbs from the sugar syrup and refrigerate in an airtight container for up to 3 weeks, or freeze for up to 1 year.

Yield: 2 cups (480 ml)

FIVE-HERB CHEESE SPREAD

This spread makes excellent tea sandwiches or a dip for party crackers and is best made several days in advance of use.

> 8 ounces (225 g) Cheddar cheese, grated, at room temperature
> ¼ cup (60 ml) dry sherry
> 2 tablespoons (30 g) sour cream or heavy cream
> 1 tablespoon (4 g) finely chopped fresh parsley
> 1 tablespoon (3 g) finely chopped fresh chives
> 1 tablespoon (2.4 g) finely chopped fresh thyme
> 1 tablespoon (2.5 g) finely chopped fresh sage
> 1 tablespoon (4.4 g) finely chopped fresh savory

In a medium bowl, thoroughly blend all the ingredients. Cover the bowl and refrigerate for several hours to combine the flavors. Bring to room temperature before serving. Refrigerate leftovers in an airtight container for up to 2 weeks.

Yield: 8 to 10 servings

ROSEMARY WALNUTS

Easy to prepare, these tasty walnuts packaged in a pretty glass jar make a thoughtful gift of "remembrance" for a friend.

1 cup (100 g) walnut halves
1 tablespoon (15 ml)
melted butter
1 teaspoon minced crushed fresh
rosemary leaves
¼ teaspoon salt
¼ teaspoon paprika

Preheat the oven to 350°F (180°C, or gas mark 4).

In a small bowl, stir together all the ingredients to coat the walnuts thoroughly. Spread the walnuts in shallow pan in a single layer. Roast until brown, about 10 minutes. Serve warm. Store leftovers in a glass jar with a tight-fitting lid at room temperature for 2 to 3 months.

Yield: 4 servings

EASY HERB MUSTARD

This tasty mustard makes a super glaze for chicken or pork and its pleasing herbal flavor complements a variety of salad and picnic dishes.

1½ cups (264 g) prepared
mustard
4½ tablespoons (67.5 g) light
brown sugar
1½ teaspoons dried sweet
marjoram
1½ teaspoons dried sweet basil
1½ teaspoons dried spearmint
1½ teaspoons crushed
coriander seeds
1½ teaspoons dried lemon
thyme leaves
¼ teaspoon celery salt
6 tablespoons (90 g) mayonnaise

In a medium bowl, stir together the mustard and brown sugar until the brown sugar dissolves.

Add the herbs and celery salt and stir to combine.

Blend the mayonnaise into the mustard mixture until well combined. Refrigerate in an airtight container for up to 1 week.

Yield: about 1 cup (about 425 g)

These herbs all blend well together and complement one another in herbal tisanes (infusions).

Basil: pleasant flavor, spicy, stimulating

Catnip: minty; soothes nerves

Lemon Balm: pleasant flavor; soothes nerves

Lemon Thyme: delectable flavor; eases headaches and nightmares

Peppermint: warming, soothing, aids digestion

Rosemary: piney, tonic, soothes nerves, aids digestion

Sage: eases coughs; general body tonic

Leaves of lemon verbena, lemon thyme, rose geranium, and mint, when added to a China tea, make it a very special treat. Note, though, that a true herbal tisane does not use China tea.

Making and Using Herbal Teas

To make herbal tea, warm a glass, earthenware, or china tea pot—never metal. Adjust the strength of the brew by the quantity of herb used. Some herbs, such as rosemary, sage, or thyme, are very strong, so use a lesser amount; for herbs such as lemon balm or marjoram, use more. Cut fresh herbs into pieces and bruise the pieces before steeping. Place fresh or dried leaves in the warmed pot: 1 teaspoon dried herbs or 1 tablespoon (weight varies) fresh herbs per 1 cup (240 ml) of water. Steep for 5 to 10 minutes. Strain and serve.

Culinary Recipes Using Your Herbal Harvest

The subtle blend of flavors is the magic of herb seasoning. The secret to using herbs successfully is moderation. Some herbs are more intensely flavored than others, especially rosemary, sage, oregano, and thyme. Others that are not so strong include sweet marjoram, basil, and mint. Learn the characteristic flavor of each herb with trial and error to find what you like best.

ROSE GERANIUM CAKE

The scented geranium leaves and strawberry jam frosting give this cake a unique fresh herbal look and flavor.

5 or 6 fresh rose geranium leaves
Any white or yellow layer or
  sponge cake batter; box cake
  works fine, too, plus the
  ingredients listed on the box
Strawberry jam, for frosting

Using your favorite cake recipe, preheat the oven according to the recipe or package instructions. Fit a sheet of wax paper into the bottom of a 9 × 13-inch (23 × 33 cm) baking dish.

Arrange several rose geranium leaves on the wax paper.

Prepare the batter as directed. Carefully pour the batter into the pan covering the geranium leaves. Bake according to the recipe instructions or package directions.

Let the cake cool somewhat before removing it from the pan to cool completely.

Remove the geranium leaves before frosting. The leaves impart a lovely taste and fragrance to the cake. Frost the cake with strawberry jam.

Yield: 9 to 10 servings

PESTO CHEESECAKE

Serve wedges of this delicious savory cheesecake on a cheese platter as an appetizer with crackers and fresh fruit. A perfect party dish.

1 tablespoon (14 g) butter
¼ cup (28 g) dried bread crumbs
2 tablespoons (12.5 g g) grated
   Parmesan cheese plus
   ½ cup (50 g)
2 (8-ounce, or 225 g) packages
   cream cheese, at room
   temperature
1 cup (250 g) ricotta
⅓ teaspoon cayenne pepper
¼ teaspoon salt
3 large eggs
½ cup (120 g) pesto
¼ cup (34 g) pine nuts
Fresh basil leaves, for garnish

Preheat the oven to 325°F (170°C, or gas mark 3). Coat the inside of 9-inch (23 cm) springform pan with the butter.

In a small bowl, stir together the bread crumbs and 2 tablespoons (12.5 g) of grated Parmesan cheese. Coat the bottom of the prepared pan with the crumb mixture.

In a medium bowl, using a handheld mixer, beat the cream cheese, ricotta, remaining ½ cup (50 g) of Parmesan cheese, cayenne, and salt until combined.

One at a time, add the eggs, beating well after each addition. Pour half the batter into another bowl and stir in the pesto. Pour the pesto mixture into the prepared pan and smooth the top. Carefully spoon the plain cheese mixture over the pesto mixture and gently smooth the top.

Sprinkle the cheesecake with pine nuts.

Bake until the center is firm and no longer moves when pan is shaken, about 45 minutes. Transfer to a cooling rack and let cool completely. Cover and refrigerate overnight.

Garnish with fresh basil leaves to serve with your favorite crackers or party rye, as desired.

Yield: 12 to 14 servings

POACHED PEARS À LA 'ROBER'S LEMON ROSE'

I must admit this recipe converted me to really enjoy eating scented geraniums. These just-barely caramelized pears are sublime on their own. 'Rober's Lemon Rose'–scented geranium gives the perfect herbal nuance to this dish, but any rose- or lemon-scented geraniums would work in its place. These pears can be adorned with whipped cream or even vanilla ice cream, if desired. Choose pears that are firm and nearly ripe— about 2 days from eating out of hand— Bartlett, Bosc, or Anjou will do.

Herb sugars are simple and inexpensive to make. Use them for sweetening tea or anywhere else you would use white sugar.

For scented geranium sugar:
2 cups (400 g) sugar
¾ to 1 cup (weight varies) clean dried rose geranium leaves, or any sweetly flavored herbs, such as lemon balm or mint

For pears:
1 lemon
4 firm, ripe pears
8 scented geranium leaves
½ cup (100 g) scented geranium sugar
¼ cup (60 ml) water

To make the scented sugar: In a clean 1-pint (480 ml) glass Mason jar with a tight-fitting lid, layer ½ inch (1 cm) or so of sugar in the bottom of the jar. Place a few scented leaves in the sugar. Add another ½-inch (1 cm) layer of sugar and layer on a few more herb leaves. Continue layering the sugar and herbs until the jar is almost full. Leave ½ inch (1 cm) or so of headspace at the top. Seal the lid and shake the jar.

Store the sugar on a cool dark shelf for 2 to 3 weeks for the flavor of the leaves to infuse the sugar. Strain the leaves out of the sugar and return the sugar to the container, seal the lid, and store indefinitely.

To make the pears: Remove the zest from the lemon in large strips. Halve the lemon and reserve one half.

Peel the pears, halve them lengthwise, and remove their cores. As you peel each pear, place the halves in in a large nonreactive sauté pan or skillet, cut-side-down, so they fit in a single layer and squeeze a little lemon juice over each pear half (use the juice of ½ lemon total). When all the pears are in the pan, scatter the lemon zest strips over the pears, place the geranium leaves in the pan, and sprinkle the sugar over everything.

Cover the pan and place it over medium heat. Cook, covered, for 7 to 8 minutes until the liquid in the pan bubbles furiously. Remove the lid and carefully turn the pears with a spatula so the round side is down. Carefully add the water to the pan, shake the pan,

and re-cover it. Cook for 7 to 8 minutes more.

Turn the pears once again, cut-side down. They may have a few golden-brown spots. Test for doneness with the tip of a knife—the pears should be tender—not mushy.

Immediately transfer the pears to a serving platter and scrape all the lovely caramel (there won't be much), lemon zest strips, and wilted geranium leaves

from the pan over the pears. If you prefer, remove the wilted leaves and garnish with fresh ones. I rather like the ones with the syrup all over them. Serve immediately, slightly warm or at room temperature.

Recipe Courtesy Susan Belsinger

Yield: 4 or 8 servings; 2 cups (400 g) scented sugar

Herbal Recipes for Personal Delight

Making beauty treatments from herbs and natural ingredients is easier than you think, especially if you grow your own herbs. All you need is herb tea, a concoction of leaves, roots, or seeds. A tea made from leaves is called an *infusion*. Simply pour boiling water over fresh or dried herb leaves and let steep for 5 to 15 minutes. A *decoction* is a tea brewed from the seeds or roots of an herb, boiled in water for 10 to 15 minutes. Plain teas can be used as a gargle, hair rinse, or skin tonic.

HERBAL HAND CREAM

People have been practicing kitchen alchemy for thousands of years and there are many variations of this herbal hand cream recipe. It is a simple mixture of oil, wax, water, and a mild alkali. Have fun experimenting with these ingredients to create a cream suited to your needs.

> ¼ cup (56.75 g) grated beeswax
> ½ cup (120 ml) olive oil
> ¼ cup (60 ml) herbal tea
> ½ teaspoon borax powder
> Tea tree essential oil

In a small saucepan over low heat, between 175°F and 185°F (79°C and 85°C), slowly warm and blend the beeswax and olive oil. As the last bits of beeswax melt into the oil, remove the pan from the heat and let sit.

In another small saucepan over medium heat, stir together the herbal tea and borax until the borax dissolves. Bring to a bare simmer.

Transfer the beeswax-oil blend into a medium bowl. Add several drops of tea tree essential oil. While whisking vigorously, mix the tea solution, one splash at a time, into the beeswax-oil blend. Continue mixing until the oil and water phases are completely incorporated.

Pour the cream into a clean 8-ounce (240 ml) container with a lid. Label and date the container and use within several months.

Yield: about 8 ounces (240 ml)

Use a little of this oil for massage, as thyme is known to sooth and relax the body. *For external use only.*

14 ounces (420 ml) almond oil
½ cup (19 g) fresh thyme leaves

Chop the thyme leaves and place them in a wide-mouth 1-pint (480 ml) jar. Pour in the almond oil, covering the leaves. Seal the lid and let steep in a sunny location for 2 weeks.

Strain and bottle the oil in a clean glass jar. Store away from bright sunlight and use within 6 months.

Yield: about 14 ounces (420 ml)

Bathing with Herbs

Herbal baths soften the skin while stimulating circulation, easing tired muscles. They can be either refreshing or relaxing depending on the herbs you choose. Put 1 cup (weight varies) fresh or dried herbs into a muslin bag and hang it from the faucet, letting the water run through the herbs as you fill the tub. Or, make a strong infusion from 1 cup (weight varies) fresh or dried herbs and 4 cups (960 ml) water and add it to the bath. Lavender, mint, patchouli, rosemary, or thyme all make a pleasant bath.

Facial Steams

A facial steam deep cleans and softens the skin. Your skin should be thoroughly clean before steaming.

Place a handful of fresh herbs in a basin and pour boiling water over them. Lean over the basin, tenting a towel over your head to keep the steam from escaping. Stream for up to 10 minutes. Rinse your face with warm water, then cool water. Pat dry. Do not steam your face more than once a week and only occasionally if your skin is dry.

Herbs for Decorative and Aromatic Delights

QUICK AND EASY POTPOURRI

Potpourri is a scented blend of dried plant materials, which includes flowers, herbs, spices, and fixatives. Blending your own potpourri to suit your individual needs and preferences is creative and fun. There are no precise rules in the choice or proportion of ingredients; creating a potpourri recipe is an art based on personal taste and discretion. You can use a recipe or follow your nose. Mixtures can depend solely on the natural scent of their ingredients, or they can be enhanced with fixatives and essential oils. Fixatives help capture and preserve the volatile oils in the herbs and flowers and prolong the life of the potpourri. Essential oils are concentrated aromatic plant distillates.

The dried herbs and spices may include flower petals or blossoms, leaves, seeds, bark, and roots. Dried citrus peel is often added for color, texture, and aroma. Whenever I have an orange or tangerine, I save the peels and dry them on a screen. I then store my dried herbs and citrus peels in glass jars until I am ready to create a fragrant concoction.

3 tablespoons (19 g) orris
  root powder
1 teaspoon essential oil
1 quart (weight varies) crisp dried
  herbs and flowers
3 tablespoons (weight
  varies) spices

In a quart-size (960 ml) glass jar, blend the orris root and essential oil. Seal the lid and let sit for a few days to allow the orris root to absorb the moisture of the oil, shaking occasionally.

In a large bowl, combine the dried flowers and herbs in any pleasing ratio, typically half herbs and half flowers. Add the orris powder mixture and blend well. Return the mixture to the jar, seal the jar, and let sit for several weeks. Package in individual jars or sachet bags for use, or gift giving.

Yield: 1 quart (weight varies)

A "talking bouquet," "word posy," or
tussie-mussie is a circular nosegay
whose fragrant herbs and flowers carry a
message in the language of flowers—of
friendship, romance, good health, or a
variety of other sentiments.

Flowers and herbs have been used
throughout the centuries to honor the
traditional customs and rituals of daily
life. In the early 1700s, the language of
flowers was introduced in England in the
form of *floriography*—the art and craft
of sending messages by flowers. At the
height of its popularity in the Victorian
era, floral dictionaries of plant meanings
topped the bestseller list.

These fragrant little bouquets make
perfect gifts for special occasions, favors
for weddings or showers, or just to say, "I
love you," to a dear friend. It's amusing
to experiment with the meanings by
including herbs such as rosemary for
remembrance, lavender for devotion,
thyme for courage and happiness, and
sage for good health. Talking bouquets
are as much fun to make and give as to
receive. If you don't feel like making a
hand bouquet, send the message in an
arrangement of fresh flowers and herbs.
It's the sentiment that counts.

Note: These little bouquets do not
require a lot of plant material; the quantity of herbs and flowers you will need
to gather depends on the size of the
bouquet you wish to create. It is always
prudent to have extra flowers and herbs
on hand. However, it is important to

condition fresh herbs and flowers before
arranging them in bouquets or floral
designs. Strip lower leaves from flowers
and herbs and place the stems in tepid
water for 6 to 8 hours—overnight is
even better.

Fresh herbs and flowers,
  as desired
Scissors
Floral wire
Florist tape
Doilies (paper or cloth)
*Liquid starch (if using a cloth
  doily), for stiffening*
Narrow ribbon, for decoration

Cutting on a diagonal, shorten the
flower and herb stems to 4 to 5 inches
(10 to 13 cm) long.

Select your single center bloom. A
rose bud is traditional but a tight bunch

of lavender or any circular flower will do. Holding the center flower in your hand, surround it with 5 or 6 sprigs of a small contrasting flower or herb. Snugly wrap florist wire around the bundle to secure it but do not cut the wire.

Add 2 or 3 more rings of herbs, securing with wire after each addition. After securing the last ring of herbs, bring the wire down the stems and push the end of the wire into the bouquets stems to fasten it.

Stretch the florist tape around the stems, from top to bottom, to form a handle.

Lastly, add a doily. If using a paper doily, cut an X in the center of the doily to slip the stems through it. If using a real cloth or lace doily, stiffen it by dipping in liquid starch and smoothing against a hard service until completely dry. Place the stems in the center of the doily or hanky and bring it up around the stems. Secure at the top with a ribbon.

Yield: 1 talking bouquet

PRESSED HERBS AND FLOWERS

People have been pressing and drying plants for centuries. It's a simple but rewarding way to preserve the beauty of herb flowers and leaves for later use. A wide variety of decorative botanical crafts are easy to make with pressed flowers, or simply tuck a fragrant leaf or pretty flower into a letter to a friend.

Sharp scissors
Large, heavy books, for weighting
Newspaper, unprinted newsprint,
  or old telephone book
Fresh flowers and leaves

Select only perfect fresh herb flowers and leaves for pressing. Pick them in different stages of development: bud, half-open, and fully open flowers and seed heads. Press some flowers in a side view, instead of open-face and bend some stems into graceful forms.

Gently arrange the plant material between layers of absorbent paper, being careful to make sure the flowers and leaves do not overlap. Pressed flowers need a warm dry environment to retain their vibrant colors. Plants that dry quickly hold their color better than plants with thicker stems, flowers, and succulent leaves.

Once dried, pressed plants are very delicate and feathery. Use a pair of tweezers to transport and arrange the pressed flowers and leaves on paper. Store in a cardboard box layered between sheets of paper.

Yield: varies

HERBAL PARCHMENT PAPER

Herbal parchment paper lends a natural twist to journal covers, greeting cards, scrapbooking projects, and Valentine's Day cards. It is simple enough to be made by youngsters but can also be used to create sophisticated papers and gift tags. Before gluing down any dried flowers, experiment with different designs of the pressed flowers and herbs on a sheet of white paper.

¼ cup (60 ml) white glue
¼ cup (60 ml water
Wax paper
Soft-bristled brush
Pressed herb flowers and leaves
Tweezers
Tissue or rice paper sheets in soft
   pastel colors
Paper towels
Steam iron
Magazines or books, for
   weighting
Metal-edged ruler

In a small bowl, stir together the glue and water, diluting the glue to a light consistency of coffee creamer.

Cut a piece of wax paper to the desired size. Brush the wax paper with the diluted glue. Place the plant material on the wax paper in the desired design. Some people find a pair of tweezers helpful when placing the dried plant materials.

Carefully cover the entire sheet of wax paper with one layer of tissue paper. Using the brush, work from the center out, gently "paint" over the tissue with the diluted glue in as few strokes as possible to avoid tearing the tissue and to eliminate air bubbles. Let dry completely.

Place the "parchment" between 2 sheets of paper towel, wax-side up. Using a warm iron, seal the parchment.

Weight the paper under a stack of magazines or books until cool to prevent curling.

Gently tear the edges of your paper on the metal edge of a ruler to give it a "soft" edge.

Resources and Suppliers

GARDENING SUPPLIES
Gardener's Supply
Containers, potting mix, seed starting supplies and more
888-833-1412
Gardeners.com

Mountain Rose Herbs
Bulk herbs
P.O. Box 50220
Eugene, Oregon 97402
MountainRoseHerbs.com

Sunlight Supply, Inc.
Wholesale grow lights and hydroponic equipment with retailers nationwide
888-478-6544
SunlightSupply.com

PLANTS AND SEEDS
Baker Creek Heirloom Seeds
2278 Baker Creek Road
Mansfield, MO 65704
RareSeeds.com

Johnny's Selected Seeds
955 Benton Avenue
Winslow, ME 04901
JohnnySeeds.com

Logee's Tropical Plants
141 North Street
Danielson, CT 06239
888-330-8038
Logees.com

Mudbrick Herb Cottage
491 Gold Coast Springbrook Road
Mudgeeraba QLD 4213 Queensland,
Australia
HerbCottage.com.au

Renee's Garden
6060 Graham Hill Road
Felton, CA 95018
888-880-7228
ReneesGarden.com

Richter's Herbs
357 Highway 47
Goodwood, ON LOC 1A0
Canada
Richters.com

Strictly Medicinal Seeds
P.O. Box 299
Williams, OR 97544
StrictlyMedicinalSeeds.com

ORGANIZATIONS
American Botanical Council
P.O. Box 144345
Austin, TX 78714-4345
Herbalgram.org

Herb Society of America
9019 Kirtland Chardon Road
Kirtland, OH 44094
HerbSociety.org

International Herb Association
P.O. Box 5667
Jacksonville, FL 32247-5667
iherb.org

National Gardening Association
Online database of plants, discussion forums, articles, gardening blogs and much more for members in the United States and Canada
Garden.org

NEW BOOKS FOR OLD GARDENERS AND OLD BOOKS FOR NEW GARDENERS

Allaway, Zia. *Indoor Edible Garden*. New York: DK Publishing, 2017.

Belsinger, Susan, and Arthur O. Tucker. *The Culinary Herbal*. Portland, OR: Timber Press, 2016.

Belsinger, Susan, and Tina Marie Wilcox. *The Creative Herbal Home*. Hollister, MO: Creative Printing & Design, 2007.

Bird, Richard. *A Gardener's Latin*. New York: William Morrow and Company, 1999.

Bown, Deni. *Encyclopedia of Herbs & Their Uses*. New York: Doring-Kindersley,1995.

Cox, Janice. *Natural Beauty at Home*. New York: Henry Holt & Company, 2002.

Foster, Steven. *Herbal Renaissance: Growing & Understanding Herbs in the Modern World*. Salt Lake City: Gibbs-Smith, 1993.

Halleck, Leslie F. *Gardening Under Lights*. Portland, OR: Timber Press, 2018.

Hessayon, D.G. *The Houseplant Expert*. London: Transworld Publishers, 2001.

Martin, Tovah. *The Unexpected Houseplant*. Portland, OR/London: Timber Press, 2012.

McCreary, Rosemary. *Tabletop Gardens*. North Adams, MA: Storey Publishing, 2006.

Mieseler, Theresa. *Beyond Rosemary, Basil, and Thyme*. Chaska, MN: Shady Acres Herb Farm, 2019.

Simmons, Adelma Grenier. *Herbs to Grow Indoors*. New York: Hawthorn Books, 1969.

Skinner, Charles M. *Myths and Legends of Flowers, Trees, Fruits, and Plants*. Philadelphia: J.B. Lippincott Co., 1911.

Acknowledgments

How does the herb become the teacher? For plants so long associated with humankind, the human voice is needed. The interpreter speaks for the herb. And there are many stories to be told.
—**Audrey O'Connor, The Herbarist 60 (1994)**

It is my pleasure and privilege to acknowledge my herbal friends and colleagues of the Herb Society of America and the International Herb Association. Their expert knowledge and thoughtful advice have been of invaluable help to me in gathering materials for this book.

Special appreciation and thanks to Caroline W. Amidon and Joyce Brobst, past presidents of The Herb Society of America—two great herbal mentors–for sharing their considerable knowledge on growing and using *Pelargoniums* indoors. I especially wish to thank Theresa Mieseler and Pat Crocker for their good sense and unfailing support over the years, in and out of the garden. "More grows in a garden than a gardener sows."

A special bouquet of thanks to the herb professionals who generously shared their expertise and recipes for this book. You have taught me much about the doctrine of herbal friendship.

* Susan Belsinger, Poached Pears à la 'Rober's Lemon Rose'
* Pat Crocker, Rose-Fruit Clafoutis
* Kathleen Gips, Scented Geranium Salad Dressing
* Donna Frawley, Lemon Geranium Mousse
* Don Haynie, Herbal Topiary Plunger
* Patricia Kenny, Pressed Flower Cards
* The Branch County Herb Questers, for all the knowledge and recipes shared over the past 35 years. Special thanks to Mary Houchen, a great cook with an extraordinary herbal touch.

My sincere gratitude and appreciation to the following plant growers for help securing many of the herbs and topiaries featured in this book: Conrad Richter, Richter Herbs; Teresa van den Hombegh, Old World Gardens; Suzanne Baker, Rush Creek Herbs; Sessile Szarafinski and Jessica Albright Wright.

Thanks to Gert Coleman and Bea Osborn for helping me organize my words and Amy Kimball for sharing my vision and love of plants in the photos artfully displayed throughout this book.

Many thanks to Jessica Walliser, editor, Cool Springs Press, for catching my pitch and sliding home with me.

About the Author

Susan Betz has been actively involved in growing and using herbs to educate the public about gardening and the natural world for more than 40 years. She is an Honorary Master Gardener, a member of the International Herb Association, Garden Communicators, the Ecological Landscape Alliance, and the National Garden Bureau. Susan is a life member of the Herb Society of America (HSA) and received The Society's Helen D. Conway Little Medal of Honor in 2018. She is a charter member of HSA's Native Herb Conservation committee, the Society's sustainable garden initiative. Susan currently serves on HSA's Notable Native Herb program and is a contributing author to HSA's native herb fact sheets published annually. She is the author of *Magical Moons & Seasonal Circles, Stepping into the Circle of the Seasons* and *Neighboring with Nature/Native Herbs for Pleasure and Purpose.*

Index